CHILDREN'S LITERATURE AND NATIONAL IDENTITY

CHILDREN'S LITERATURE AND NATIONAL IDENTITY

edited by Margaret Meek

Trentham Books

Stoke on Trent, UK and Sterling, USA

Trentham Books Limited

Westview House	22883 Quicksilver Drive
734 London Road	Sterling
Oakhill	VA 20166-2012
Stoke on Trent	USA
Staffordshire	
England ST4 5NP	

First published 2001

British Library Cataloguing-in-Publication Data

A catalogue record for this book is available from the British Library
ISBN: 1 85856 204 X

Designed and typeset by Trentham Print Design Ltd., Chester and printed in Great Britain by Cromwell Press Ltd., Wiltshire.

CONTENTS

Acknowledgement
The authors of this book are those who wrote the chapters. To bring it into being I have been continuously grateful for their patience, as for the outstanding editorial skill of Gillian Klein, and the help and encouragement of my colleagues in the British section of IEDPE. MM

PREFACE

This book about children's literature and its readers stems from a colloquium held in London in the autumn of 1998 under the aegis of the European Institute for the Development of Potential in All Children. IEDPE is a European collaborative network of teachers, researchers, scholars and others responsible for the social growth and intellectual development of *all* children. Earlier meetings resulted in comparative studies of parental involvement in the beginnings of literacy, and accounts of the lives of 'hidden' children of immigrants and guest workers moving across Europe. This third colloquium included writers, researchers, publishers and, particularly, translators of children's books, so that, in the forum discussions, the importance of national identity as a shared concern became evident. Consequently, there was general agreement that the discussion documents and other relevant studies should be more conveniently available.

Here, a group of specialists addresses common themes from different cultural perspectives in order to explore how children's literature, considered as the books that children read, contributes to children's coming to know who they are in the terms of the social sameness and difference that constitute 'national identity'. When do British children know that they are British? What is it that makes the Englishness of English children's books distinct from the Frenchness of books for French children? What happens when Germans appear in French or English books? Who are the heroes and who the villains in historical novels for the young? Is stereotyping any less prevalent nowadays, or do traditional antagonisms persist? Can we blame the books that children read for the continuation of old prejudices, including racism and nationalism? Given the linguistic diversity of Europe, what part does translation play in weakening cultural boundaries? These and other questions come to the fore once the matter of 'national identity' is approached.

The scope for discussion of the issues raised is wider than the contents of this book. We have chosen to focus our inquiries on literature where children are the implied readers rather than to add another volume to the laden shelves of cultural and psychological studies. We hope, however, to see how adults who tell children stories may also reveal to them something about themselves and about a particular way of seeing the world, so that young readers may widen their view of both their individuality and their social sense of 'belonging'. Thus it is with great admiration for the specialist writers of these essays that the editor expresses gratitude for their generosity and patience in letting their work appear in this format. The rest of this introduction is simply intended to indicate some of the ideas that can be traced through each of the self-contained chapters.

Identity, as national

Identity is a shifting, slithering concept, one of the words we use to distinguish ourselves from others and then to confirm each self as unique and unified. While we acknowledge our common humanity, we also proclaim the singularity and differences of individuals in terms of where they were born and where they now choose to live. A birth certificate, an identity card or a passport give us both personal and national identity. They allow us to cross frontiers and become strangers in other places with an official attachment to our place of origin. Identity also includes notions of the self that imply our historical-cultural being. These tokens of identity are circumscribed by whatever meaning we give to 'national', an equally unstable construct which had its origins in Europe no earlier than the nineteenth century.

At some point in childhood, children discover the name of the location, country, city, town or village where they are 'at home'. This recorded address becomes an extension of themselves in a world of people they know. I recall how, aged about seven, I wrote my name on the cover of a new notebook, and then added the name of the street and the town. I continued with 'The Kingdom of Fife, Scotland, Great Britain, the British Isles, Europe, the World'. At about the same time I learned to recite this verse by Walter Scott:

Breathes there the man with soul so dead,
That never to himself hath said,
    This my own, my native land,
Whose heart hath ne're within him burned
As home his footsteps he hath turned
    From wandering in a foreign strand!

I discovered the title, *Patriotism* and the exclamation mark when I sought out the poem to write it here.

During my time in school, Scottishness was emphasised in history lessons about a warring oligarchy, the Reformation, and the malevolence of the English. Our allies were the French. Ancient ballads, the poems of Robert Burns, novels by Scott and R.L. Stevenson and the encircling Protestantism confirmed my national allegiance. The smooth speech and modified vowels of the Southerners I heard on the 'wireless' were said to be 'soft'. After more than 50 years of living in England my attachment to my early culture is still strong, but regarded differently from the 'foreign strand'. As Terry Eagleton suggests in *The Idea of Culture*, 'Membership of the tribe thus yields to citizenship of the world' (1999, p58). Different allegiances occur by turns in the lives of most people, but the early ones have a defining aspect. The 'where' of identity settles us early. Forced uprooting is known to be confusing.

National identity, commonly regarded, is a stylistic way of identifying differences between 'us' and 'others', chiefly in terms of origins, optings and associations. Strong identifications are difficult to change, especially if they have territorial attachments. Consider how difficult it is proving for people to regard themselves as 'Europeans', to consider changing the local currency, to think of distances in kilometres or about driving on the right. Part of our individuality resides in the way we fill up words with our experiences and feelings, as when we respond to 'exile', 'refugee', 'immigrant', 'travel' and 'homeless'.

As I read this collection of papers, I saw that the complexities of self-identification, national, social and psychological, are well inscribed in the writers' examples. Then, as these things happen at times of heightened consciousness, I found a pertinent protocol for the relation of national identity with literature in an exhibition of selected manuscripts, entitled 'Chapter and Verse', ('the sheer diversity of our literary heritage'), in the British Library. It is divided under headings that relate to the dominant concerns of our inner lives as portrayed in literature: love and loss, time and place, humour and imagination, faith and identity, belonging and conflict. Children's books are well to the fore, as is their distinctive Englishness.

In the first display case, entitled *Identity,* is an original copy of King Alfred's ninth century preface to his translation of Pope Gregory's instructions in Latin to his sixth century clergy. The accompanying note describes King Alfred as 'a pioneering writer of prose' who 'implored his subjects to learn English in order to re-establish a sense of cultural and intellectual identity after the ravages of the Vikings. His efforts helped to establish the language of a literary inheritance'. By giving his readers an English version of an important Latin text, he could 'begin to establish a sense of national identity'. Nearby is *The Book of Margery Kempe* (1373-1439) ' the oldest extant autobiography in the English language' (discovered in 1944), with this reason for its inclusion in this section of the exhibition, 'Explorations of what makes us who we are (or who we think we are) have since then provided literature with some of its most important themes'. National identity is undoubtedly linked with language; children learn their culture as they learn to speak. In retrospect, we attribute the modern notion of national identity to the writers of these early texts because we discern certain continuities in word meanings.

Our topic clearly has a long history and, equally clearly, changes over time. Here now is a contemporary occurrence of our theme. In Amit Chaudhuri's recent novel, *A New World*, the hero, Jayojit, now established in the affluence of the Midwest of the United States, goes back to Calcutta to visit his parents and thus to revisit his own childhood and youth.

> It was at that time, the Admiral remembered, that the question of what it was to be an 'Indian' had had to be addressed. It was not something that either Jayojit or Admiral Chatterjee had bothered about, except during moments of political crises or significance, like a border conflict or elections or some movement of mass celebrations, when it seemed all right to mock 'Indianness', if only to differentiate oneself from a throng of people. (p.90)

Our concerns do not take us into the topic of political identity, but clearly this is also relevant. If we agree that literature offers and encourages a continuing scrutiny of 'who we think we are', we have to emphasise the part that children's literature plays in the development of children's understanding of both belonging (being one of us) and differentiation (being other). In the outside world, children adopt adult attitudes that their books either confirm or challenge. The British experience of making children's books multicultural so that all children could 'see themselves' in them is our best example of how critical insistence that fiction for children should reflect social realities brought about changes in publishing practices. The effects, however, have been more local than transnational, another reason for wider sharing of common experiences.

Culture, as multicultural

In 1976, Raymond Williams said that 'culture is one of the two or three most complex words in the English language' (*Keywords* p.57). Since then, most humane studies have included definitions and examples of this complexity in their grounded theory. Williams' disciple, Terry Eagleton, quotes this sentence, then continues with masterly clarity to bring different versions of culture up to date. His last paragraph includes the topics addressed here: 'Culture is not only what we live by. It is also, in great measure, what we live for. Affection, relationship, memory, kinship, place, community, emotional fulfilment, intellectual enjoyment, a sense of ultimate meaning; these are closer to us than charters of human rights or trade treaties' (p.131). These aspects of our lives are also the stuff of literature. We could make different but comparable lists of the desires of young people who are looking forward to adventures they will find in books as well is in the world. Words come to them laden with overtones of significance as they begin to talk, to read and write. Are not these stages in the formation of their cultural/national identity?

Local cultures are the strongest social bonds. In most people they establish unconscious conformity and allegiance. Language is an obvious cohesive factor everywhere. New arrivals who don't speak as the people around them do provoke local racisms. Refugees, guest workers and other immigrants are welcomed for their skills, but are often disparaged when they keep their traditional cultural habits of language, food and dress. They may then move closer than ever to each other. In absorbing adult attitudes, children may learn to distrust strangers because they adopt what they recognise as normal or usual in different groupings, religious and ethnic ones in particular. Boundary crossing is difficult. We know it is important to help children to distinguish ethnic identity from political nationalism, but these distinctions are complex for the young.

There are also confusions about what counts as a 'national' tradition. For example, the United Kingdom has no specially marked national day as many other nations have, such as the fourth of July in the USA or the fourteenth of July in France. November 11, Armistice Day, had a temporary revival. Empire Day, Trafalgar Day and the Queen's birthday were once special event days in the calendar but they now pass virtually unnoticed, except for the flags flying on public buildings. There are ceremonial events associated with royalty: the opening of Parliament is one, but this is not a togetherness occasion. In stark contrast, Northern Ireland is riven by conflicting versions of what is claimed to be national identity, but these topple into political nationalism. Oppressed minorities and 'freedom fighters' claim national distinction. Some sense of national identity remains in countries where young men still do compulsory military service. Career soldiers are bound to adopt the identity that comes with their uniform. I have seen no recent, definitive depictions of sailors, soldiers or airmen in modern English books for the very young, although this was not so when Biggles was widely read.

There is, however, ample evidence of a continuing concern that British children's books should reflect the multicultural nature of our society. The first *Multicultural Guide to Children's Books* appeared in 1985. By 1994 Rosemary Stones could report that there had been 'the emergence of a new generation of British born black poets and writers whose work speaks authoritatively to a young audience for whom multicultural realities are, by and large, taken for granted'.

In the millennium edition of the *Guide*, Farruk Dhondy explains multi-culturalism as a 'post colonial, a new European idea', the result of 'the movement and settlement of people'. This part of his argument is wholly relevant to the contents of this book:

> This confounding of multiculturalism with anti-racism is understandable, but it is the merest of contemporary coincidences and a serious mistake.
>
> Anti-racism is a simple and self-evident creed, however many skirmishes remain to be fought on its terrain.
>
> As an idea, multiculturalism is transnational and it has nothing essential to do with race. Its first law is that cultures clash. Its second law is that cultures may clash in one and the same person and can do so with spectacular literary results. (p.116)

Authors who are challenged by these complexities and paradoxes write books that may not only reveal children to themselves, but can also offer glimpses of others in the same multicultural world. This notion is well rehearsed here in relation to the European scene.

Translation and transition

Language is at the heart of any discussion of national identity. Ordinary folk define themselves by the language or languages they speak. Bilingualism is normal, common, in countries with land frontiers. Dialects separate British Islanders both regionally and in terms of class distinctions. 'Standard' English is sometimes more divisive than unifying; suspicion is more common than trust. Many problems of babeldom remain; increase even, in a world where successful and fast communications are all-important.

As the result of colonial conquests, the power of American film and TV industries, travel and dominant banking, English has become the *lingua franca* for global transactions and exchanges. In Europe, more successful efforts have been made to teach schoolchildren a second language, usually English. No comparable results have been noted in native English speakers with regard to other European languages, still called 'foreign'. The monolingual state of most people in the UK is not the best beginning for multicultural awareness in children. When I hear people announce their satisfaction that English is now the world language, I am apt to say that this also means that English-only speakers can understand less than half of what is being said. English also penetrates other languages. No translation is needed for the lyrics of popular songs. This movement to multicultural recognition of diversity as well as unity in Europe makes monolinguals seem isolationist.

Translation from one language into another has evolved, in nature and in use, from classical scholarly erudition and notions of 'correctness' into a wide range of interpretive linguistic practices. The most obvious changes are in the translation of speech, notably in high-level political encounters and meetings, where the skill of instantaneous translators has become the model for success for all. As in all conversations, understanding is best in a shared context. Delegates to the United Nations who wear headphones when the speaker's language is unfamiliar to them, are listening for the emphasis and tone of the utterance as much as for its content, which they may already know about from a written memo.

Written translation is one of the core issues of this book. Here we see that it is not a language-changing facility. Instead it is part of the art and craft of writing, with a long history in both ancient and modern languages. Contemporary poets re-translate Ovid's *Metamorphoses* and *Beowulf* so that others can read and understand their contemporary relevance. We should know less of the great cultures of the world if versions and interpretations of their important texts had not been made available in other languages. The craft of translation lies in the translator's knowledge of both the original text and its context, and the appropriate presentational forms in the target language. The art is in the way the translator does felicitous justice to the feelings, overtones and subtleties of *both* languages. Many of the writers in this book have practised these skills with notable success.

Authors who have written in English, whether for adults or children, from a country where they have chosen to work and to live, demonstrate what Gabriel Josipovici calls 'the link between exile and linguistic innovation'. He has in mind writers like Joyce, Becket and Nabokov, who have enriched the English language and extended its literature. Salman Rushdie's book for the young, *Haroun and the Sea of Stories* is also a work of this kind. We can and should expect more intercultural writing as authors realise the concern of modern children to explore childhood away from home.

Again, it becomes clear that complex topics of language and literature in translation extend to books and other texts designed for children. The obligation of this preface is to suggest that we should not accept without question the claim that translations of children's books that originate outside English-speaking countries are too expensive to be profitable. This is more an excuse than a justification for the lack of trade in translated texts, especially in Europe. Books in English reach the biggest market. Books translated into English could have their share of it. The view of writers in this book is that readers of English cannot afford to be isolationist in the world of literature for children.

Children's books

An acknowledged conviction about children's books in the UK is that they should be a pleasure for their readers. Although the aesthetic and intellectual content of these manifold productions varies widely, the overall standard of writing and design is linked to the intention that children should enjoy reading if they are to become confident and competent literates. In infancy, children have books as toys to be handled and looked at. Innocent as they seem, these are cultural objects with a didactic thrust to make children familiar with colours, letters, familiar objects and animals as words and as representational forms as soon as possible. In England, learning to read now begins very early. Different contributors make comparisons of cultural and literary forms of children's first books. Quite a number admired contemporary picture book artists, whose individual talents are discussed by critics in terms of image, text and ideology, have produced an alphabet book, a genre with a long history. A European collection of these would reveal whether or not the simplest images are invested with 'national' distinctions.

Picture books are windows on a cultural context. *The Baby's Catalogue* by Janet and Allan Ahlberg invites the youngest of readers to recognise the familiar events and objects in child-rearing practices in the UK in 1982. Five families with common needs and social habits are distinguished by their daily engagements with breakfasts, games, shopping, gardens, accidents, dinners, mirrors, pets, baths and bedtimes. Under each headword are pictures that present the range of social differences that are assumed to be ordinary The latent sense of sameness and difference is interpreted by 'insiders', while those outside the cultural familiarity of class distinctions interpret the book as a whole as a typically English depiction of childhood. As usual, the work has a dual readership in mind. Adults see the sociological aspects of the differences. Recent research by Penni Cotton and her colleagues has pursued inquiries into sameness and difference by using a range of European texts in different countries, some of which she has included here.

National identity in children's books is part of cultural distinctions. Occasionally, however, it is foregrounded, nostalgically, as in Michael Foreman's autobiographical picture book, *War Boy, a Country Childhood* and in *Peepo*, the Ahlbergs' book-as-toy, where the reader follows the baby's glance through the spy-hole in the pages to see the details of the parents' lives in 1940.

Meanwhile, it is interesting to look at another characteristic example of national identity latent in a book that uses the literature of childhood to produce an ironic, modern polysemic text to engage the dual readership of children and adults; the Ahlbergs again. In *The Jolly Postman*, English nursery rhyme characters are combined with contemporary events and literary conventions, so that readers can read 'other people's letters'. This book has a worldwide readership. The 'Englishness' seems to be part of the attraction: the rural scenery, the eccentricities of the characters and the collecting up in the layered text of familiar English story conventions. Just how books 'travel' is a concern for publishing houses in the promotion and distribution that has always been at the heart of the children's market. It would be interesting to know how cultural and national conventions are not only translated but also interpreted in other countries, both English and non-English-speaking, in what Maria Nicholayeva calls 'the zone of mutual understanding and translatability'(p.29).

Most national collections of children's book have historical novels. Wars and other conflicts provide ready-made plots of conflict between 'them and us'. In 1949, Geoffrey Trease protested about the narrow view of history that characterised fiction for British children, saying that their views of the English Civil War and the French Revolution were hopelessly one-sided. Of the Civil War he said that eight out of ten people in England at that time simply wanted the battles to stop, and he blamed the royalist sympathies of Baroness Orczy for the anti-revolution bias of English readers.

National identity in children's books has come to the fore in the generation of children born after the great conflicts of the twentieth century. Wars provide the classic version of 'them and us'. What we tell our children and grandchildren can now be shared with others, in Europe and elsewhere, whose interpretations of events may not be the same as our own. Recently, Carol Fox and a group of European colleagues conducted an international inquiry into the contents of books for children about war. They have produced an annotated bilingual selection containing 200 of the books available in Dutch, Portuguese and English. The rationale for this enterprise includes the EU ideology about 'transforming Europe from a theatre of war to an economic region of peaceful coexistence and co-operation'. The editors also write about the need to record the past before the eyewitnesses disappear, and to write for children about the realities of the Holocaust, for example – that 'former generations would have deemed unsuitable for them'. The range and depth of this list bring a new dimension to our topic.

Fox continues, 'the project partners are convinced that literature is a powerful medium for communicating to children what war is, what it is like, what it means and what its consequences are. In this respect the project is not an ideological or moral enterprise but a literary one'. The focus is on the content of the books rather than on the ways of telling. As a result, this is an important ground-clearing work across a wide range of fictive writing with the common theme of goodies and baddies. It shows the opportunity offered by literature, not only children's, for the reader to consider another point of view, and even the prospect of reconciling different viewpoints. A common theme that emerges from the EU report and the contents of this book is how authors, in writing for young people, engage the readers' allegiance to the characters. Critical readers look to see if this allegiance is well founded and not propaganda or special pleading.

The approaches to children's literature in the chapters that follow break new ground in our understanding of the need to diminish ethnocentrism. Authors who live in one country and work in another, critics whose language skills are founded on different cultural experiences of childhood, and publishers who have already taken risks to put translated books on their list have all done much to overcome insularities. We lack reports and substantial analyses of children reading translated books that have different renderings of common experiences. How is growing up in England seen from Amsterdam?

Important for me is the need to include reading whole books, not selected passages only, in the teaching of a second language to British children. While it is important for them to learn how to travel, shop and converse about everyday things using another language, continuous reading of a whole book, preferably a good modern one not designed to teach grammar and vocabulary, makes the culture more familiar and the characters less stereotypical. Conversational exchanges between characters, for example, carry the action instead of serving as exemplary sentences for translation exercises. We still need to extend the range of books we read *with* children which present a cultural context that is unfamiliar. In this way we can not only reduce the unfamiliarity but also make what is familiar less stable, more inclusive of difference.

In writing this I have become ever more acutely aware that children's books are often examples of special pleading by adults. Here no case is being made in favour of or against what is called national identity, but there is concern that, in Europe at least, we could be much clearer about how to discern common interests and to lessen prejudice and intolerance. If that can be done with greater insight into the role of books in the lives of young people then we could strive for more shared understandings.

An earlier encounter with the international study of children's books was in reading Maria Nikolajeva, who wrote that 'with very few exceptions, children's literature in different countries has little in common', and that, as 'the share of children's books occupied by translations is tending to decrease, and foreign books have great difficulties competing with national texts', children's literature in general was becoming 'more and more isolated.' Her solution is that adults must 'maintain the rightful place of children's literature in society, in education, in literary criticism. Only then can children's literature become an important part of the world cultural legacy'. That was in 1996. Whether or not our isolationism has changed will become evident to the reader of the following chapters.

Margaret Meek

PART ONE
Boundary Crossings

In order to surmount the limits of the familiar, young people need writers and artists who can take them on journeys of the mind and the imagination. In opening up our topic, Gillian Lathey shows how this is done by 'immigrating authors' and 'transnational critics' whose work reflects their own crossings of boundaries. She also demonstrates the instability of notions of what is 'national' for those who are at home in more than one country. Here the reader gains a more particular understanding of the historical, linguistic and economic matters that confront Europeans as they try to know each other better, and of the part children's literature plays in this.

The complexities of text translation are at the heart of our concerns. Here we approach them with Emer O'Sullivan. Her linguistic acuity lets us come close up to the problems of rendering *Alice in Wonderland* in German, while keeping the word play and humour of the original. Throughout this engaging, scholarly analysis we discover just how elusive are the voices of the narrator and the characters, and how culture-specific are the textual references to other books in the classical English canon. Will German readers understand Carroll's playful subtleties and know that the words usually mean more than they say, or even the opposite? This unique, rich account of the challenge offered by the children's story best known outside the English-speaking world shows how the book carries with it, as a distinctive tone, an influential picture of Englishness. Thus we see how translators become co-creators of the original, and how translation, like all other aspects of children's literature, is subject to the conditions of culture and history.

No one knows this better than Anthea Bell, whose fame as a translator is world-wide. English readers associate her with the outstanding success of Asterix. Here she offers us glimpses of her work, notably its boundary-crossing activities. As we learn more about the powerful influence of the translator who reads texts through the eyes and thoughts of the authors in order to make meaning transparent, we realise how important, and liberating, it is to be at home in more than one language.

The writers of these three chapters have a common concern about the isolation of English children's literature in 'something of a ghetto'. Although books in English are translated into many languages, there is a definite shortage of English versions of the best books that originate elsewhere. In all children's literature the dominant factor is the economics of production and distribution. The skills of skilled readers and translators: linguistic, intellectual and imaginative, deserve more general recognition, not least for their contribution to transcultural understanding.

The road from Damascus: children's authors and the crossing of national boundaries

Gillian Lathey

S elda is flying with her mother and two sisters from lzmir in western Turkey to Istanbul, en route for Switzerland to join her father and older brothers who already live there. On the hot, crowded plane Selda's attention is drawn to the non-Turkish tourists, the kind of people she will meet in her future life in northern Europe. She is as amused and puzzled by the 'undressed, sunburnt skin' of her fellow-passengers as she is by their holiday clothing:

> Beside Selda an old lady who was as white-haired as her grandmother was wearing bright pink trousers and a T-shirt. When she sat back in her seat, Selda saw that the T-shirt was printed with a mouse sunbathing under a palm tree. Those were children's clothes, surely? (p.20)

Selda is startled by the garishness and playful motifs in an elderly woman's outfit, a mode of dress which does not seem compatible with the dignity and sobriety of old age. This tiny observation is the first of many in Gaye Hiçyilmaz's novel *The Frozen Waterfall* (1993) which cause the reader to pause and reconsider unquestioned customs and values through an outsider's eyes. Such cultural jolts mark the crossing of borders in time or space, so that in the course of the novel Selda, and the reader, are frequently surprised by her encounters with the Swiss. Not only does Selda form an unlikely, awkward yet important friendship with a Swiss classmate, but the responses of individual members of her family to the consumerism and values of contemporary Switzerland differ widely. Insights into the process of adaptation to a new life, which are as subtle as they are unexpected, can only result from close observation and participation. As someone who has lived in Switzerland and who spent many years living in Turkey when she married into a Turkish family, Hiçyilmaz's personal experience combines with her ability to identify and express the telling moments of transition to make her novel one of the most realistic, precise, and sensitivity written of its kind.

The Frozen Waterfall is by language and publication a British novel, yet the intimate view of Turkish family life, the Turkish and Swiss settings and the experience of cultural change raise questions about the concept of national literatures. Is language, geography, or thematic content the touchstone by which the national allegiance of a work should be measured? If language is the key, as in Hiçyilmaz's novels (and those she writes under the name Annie Campling), what of Tove Jansson, creator of the Moomins, who is a Swedish-speaking and writing Finn? Anyone who seeks to define 'national' in such cases is likely to run into the sand of endless qualifications to any conclusions reached or, worse, to court the reductive nonsense and mythology sometimes attached to the concept of national identity. The concept of national literature is undoubtedly problematic.

Maria Nikolajeva (1996) addresses the issue when discussing the gradual divergence of national children's literatures within Europe. She defines the term 'national' as geographical rather than linguistic (leading, presumably, to a classification of Tove Jansson's books as Finnish rather than Swedish), and as oppositional. Thus Swedish children's literature can be defined in opposition to Norwegian and Danish children's literature; to West European children's literature; to American children's literature and so on. She argues that what is regarded as typically Swedish in children's books will be different when regarded from the perspective of a Norwegian, or from that of a British commentator reading a translation. Just as Maria Nikolajeva herself has brought the insights of a Russian reader to Scandinavian children's literature – the eager response to the anarchy of Astrid Lindgren's Pippi Longstocking or the subversive pranks of Karlsson within the constraints of Soviet Russia, for example – so the appreciation of what is 'national' about the children's literature of a particular country constantly changes.

Although Nikolojeva's argument illuminates the relativity of the term 'national' when applied to children's literature, it rests on the movement of books across national borders via translation, and cannot therefore easily be applied to those authors whose work reflects their own crossing of boundaries. Since the work of migrating authors stems from two or more sets of literary traditions, social mores and national histories, the kind of alternative perspectives Nikolajeva cites are already encoded within the texts themselves, as is certainly the case in *The Frozen Waterfall*. This is what makes these writers so different: they write against the grain of 'national' expectations from inside or outside their country of residence, and are able to combine elements of two cultures and their meeting points into an artistic whole. The following consideration of authors whose work springs from a sense of cultural duality reveals just what children might gain from these linguistic and imaginative acts of translation.

Literary migration may result from past colonial and economic connections or historical turning points. A loving backward glance to childhoods spent in the Caribbean (John Agard, Grace Nichols, James Berry) enhances British poetry and prose for children, just as Andrée Chedid, a French children's author born in Egypt, continues to draw on her Egyptian childhood in fiction for all ages. The terrors of war or repressive regimes send children's as well as adult writers into exile: picture book author Judith Kerr (*Mog the Forgetful Cat*, 1970) came to England as a Jewish child refugee from the Third Reich and has written for children about that experience (*When Hitler Stole Pink Rabbit*, 1971). In the post-war years economic migration such as the employment of Turkish guest workers in Germany and Switzerland which underpins *The Frozen Waterfall*, is beginning to change the nature of German language children's literature. There are now several contemporary authors writing in German who are of Turkish origin: both Yuksel Pazarkaya and the late Fakir Baykurt have written children's books about establishing a new life in Germany.

Large-scale migrations or historical connections are, however, not the only catalysts for trans-national influences in children's fiction; writers are also drawn into new areas and fruitful collaboration through personal ties. Just as Hiçyilmaz's marriage took her to Turkey, Joan Lingard's took her – albeit vicariously – to postwar Latvia. Lingard has written two novels (*Tug of War*, 1989, and *Between Two Worlds,* 1991) based on her Latvian husband's travels and emigration as a young refugee, books which introduce young British readers to the devastation and chaos of continental Europe at that time. The traumas of refugee childhood had no doubt been told and retold to Lingard over many years before the time was right for her to rework them in fictional form. A happier set of circumstances surrounds the unique novels for young people written partly in English and partly in German by Emer O'Sullivan and Dietmar Rösler. Both academics, they met when they were students at Berlin University. In the first novel of the series, *I like you – und du?* (1983), the teenage narrators, Karin from Berlin and Paddy from Ireland, tell their own love story and that of their parents – his widowed mother and her divorced father – in their respective first languages. The attraction of language lessons in fictional form, the Irish and German settings, and the focus on contemporary teenage relationships – couched in the linguistic and cultural surprises and misunderstandings the two authors understand so well – has ensured continuing high sales figures for the books in Germany.

Whatever their origins, cultural transitions in children's books are as infinitely varied as the lives of those who write about them. One writer whose remarkable story reveals an intricate web of cross-cultural connections is the Syrian

Rafik Schami, who is now one of the leading contemporary German language children's authors. Schami's fiction for both adults and children has won many prizes (the Swiss 'La vache qui lit' and a prize awarded by German national television) and is translated into more than twenty languages, including English (*A Handful of Stars,* 1991). Schami, whose adopted name means 'friend from Damascus', grew up as part of a minority Christian community in Syria and emigrated to Germany in 1971 at the age of twenty-five. Schami's exile was not part of a wider migration; he chose to leave Damascus when the authorities suppressed the subversive newspaper he edited and his freedom as a writer was under threat. Schami is above all a passionate storyteller, who emphasises the combination of oral and literary traditions in his work – indeed he insisted in an autobiographical lecture delivered in Frankfurt (*Hürdenlauf,* 1996) that he does not regard himself as a writer for children or adults, but rather as a storyteller for all ages. It is this gift which has enabled him success-fully to integrate the narrative traditions of the Arabic world with the linguistic and cultural heritage of his adopted European home.

Schami's induction into Arabic narrative and poetic traditions began early. As a child he enjoyed and quickly mastered games of poetic repartee fashioned by his father, a skill which Schami honed when learning by heart classical poetry (thirty pages at a time!) for recitation before his astonished classmates at school. Then came a momentous turning point: Radio Cairo's decision to broadcast every one of Scheherazade's one thousand and one stories, one each night over two years and eight months. Unfortunately the broadcasts did not begin until eleven thirty at night, so Schami struck a bargain with his mother. He would go to bed obediently every night at the early hour of seven, if she would wake him later so that they could listen together to each episode in the dark of a sleeping household. Schami describes in *Hürdenlauf* his difficulty in finding sleep after such a firing of his imagination. He lay in bed inventing alternative endings to the stories he had just heard, while the resolution slowly formed in his mind to enable others to share the joy of those story-filled nights. There was no doubt now about his career: until his exile Schami wrote surrealist texts, fairy tales and plays as well as newspaper articles.

For some time after his arrival in Germany in 1971, Schami wrote in Arabic and translated his own work into German; he did not begin to write directly in German until 1977. This transition period is significant in view of the in-fluence of the cadences, rhythms and conventions of Arabic oral literature on Schami's German prose, since only a gradual letting go of the first language as an artistic medium made such integration possible. In all his German publications Schami's talent as a storyteller is predominant, whether in the narrative recreation of his Syrian adolescent political activity in diary form in *A Handful of Stars* (first German edition 1987); in the traditional form of the stories in *Erzähler der Nacht* (Storytellers of the night, 1989), or in the regret at the disappearance of folk stories expressed in the picture book Schami wrote in collaboration with the illustrator Peter Knorr, *Der Wunderkasten* (The box of delights, 1990). In this story-within-a-story, the 'box' of the title is a peep-show carried by an itinerant Syrian storyteller. Four children can sit on a folding bench and watch through peep-holes in the beautifully decorated box as the storyteller unwinds a continuous roll of pictures and entertains them with the accompanying narrative. It is a story which story begins in traditional Arabic style, for the heroine, Leila, is described as: 'more beautiful than a rose and more graceful than a gazelle' (p.4).

Schami's point in this narrative is brought into sharp focus when the story of Sami the shepherd boy and his beautiful Leila is told again many years later, and we see the less than benign influence of western culture. Now the storyteller has become an old man in a Damascus full of tourists and dominated by advertising hoardings. Symbolic of this change is the roll of illustrations in the box; these are faded and damaged and the storyteller has replaced them with cuttings from magazine advertisments. Thus the country girl Leila becomes the lovely 'Kolgata', a Marilyn Monroe lookalike holding a tube of toothpaste, one of the many examples of inappropriate images sellotaped over missing portions of the original roll. Of even greater significance for Schami is the fact that these new pictures also alter the story. Names change; transistor radios, aeroplanes, painkillers and other accidental details of the adverts have to be incorporated into the narrative and accounted for in descriptive passages and new subplots. So the structure and rhythms of the original story are lost. It is this passing of the poetry of the storyteller that Schami mourns in *Hürdenlauf,* pointing out that – in contrast to most western countries – only fifty percent of the population of the Arabic speaking world at best has access to the beauty of the Arabic language via the written word. As a metaphor for the inevitability of historical changes in oral narratives and a questioning of some aspects of western influence in the Arabic world, *Der Wunderkasten* is a picture book *tour de force.*

Schami's recent publication crystallises both the patterns which have shaped his own life and his faith in literature as a medium for a more positive exchange of ideas between east and west. *Der geheime Bericht über den Dichter Goethe* (The secret report on the poet Goethe, 1999), written in collaboration with German children's author Uwe-Michael Gutzschhahn, is a utopian fantasy which whets the young reader's appetite for the work of Germany's greatest poet. Its setting, however, is the small island of Hulm in the Persian Gulf, where the islanders' idyllic and peaceful existence is threatened by oil-hungry superpowers. After much thought, the young Sultan Hakim Ben Zaki Chaligi decides that the best policy is one of openness towards the inevitable influx of western culture. So that young people on the island will learn to know and meet western strangers with confidence, he sends ten scholars abroad to discover the most important European poets and philosphers for inclusion on the syllabi of schools and universities. The establishment of a 'house of wisdom' where translators can enjoy dignity, comfort and intellectual exchange will, he hopes, ensure that the work of the selected poets reaches its audience in the best possible form.

After a year spent in Germany, a young scholar, Tuma, tries to beguile a commission of the island's leading academics into accepting Goethe into the pantheon of poets to be read by the young. He devotes nine evenings (echoes of Scheherazade!) to different aspects of Goethe's life and work, conveying the essence of each play, novel or poem in narratives tailored by authors Schami and Gutschhahn to appeal to a young audience. The audience of scholars listening to Tuma each night is delighted to discover parallels with poets of the Arabic world, as well as the delicacy, breadth, playfulness and child-like receptiveness of Goethe's imagination. A high point of Tuma's performance is his discussion and reading of poems from Goethe's *Der westöstliche Divan* (literally: the west-east collection). This exuberant collection of poems, written when Goethe was almost seventy, was inspired by translations into German of the work of the medieval Persian poet Hafiz. Thus Tuma's introduction of a western poet to his Arabic audience is a reflection of Goethe's respectful adoption of a poet from the east as a model. Goethe's reading of Hafiz, as expressed in a mixture of imitation and playful irony, confirms the growing enthusiasm of the Sultan's commission. Schami and Gutschhahn have created a parallel interchange: the meeting of minds which took place in the past between Goethe and Hafiz is echoed, many years later, by the fictional encounter between Goethe's work and Tuma's Arabic audience. It is this continuing dialogue between eastern and western traditions on which Schami and Gutschhahn focus their readers' attention, although the narrative framework of *Der geheime Bericht* presents a timely reminder of western self-interest in political contacts with the Arab world.

To which national literature, then – given his expression of Arabic traditions and concerns in the German language – does Schami's work belong? The inadequacies and limitations of national categorisation are as pertinent when discussing this Syrian-German as they were in relation to the artistry of Gaye Hiçilmaz or Joan Lingard, since in each case literary, cultural and linguistic traditions have undergone a unique process of fusion. In view of this impasse and in a year of celebrations to mark the two hundred and fiftieth anniversary of Goethe's birth, it is perhaps timely to return to his coinage of the term 'world literature'[1]. World literature did not mean for Goethe a levelling of the kind Schami warns against in *Der Wunderkasten,* but a process of exchange which would render the notion of national literature obsolete. Although Goethe's vision now seems both naive and questionable and did not take into account the economic and cultural imperialism which was to follow, he did at least voice a commitment to trans-national literature. And, in *Der west-östliche Divan*, he made a contribution to a body of literature for children and adults which stands apart from the broadbased cultural and economic exchanges of books which take place at an international level.

A literature already exists which transcends national boundaries because of the commitment and openness of individuals who have crossed borders in body or spirit throughout history. Even in the twentieth century, travel is not essential to international exchange; insights develop over many years of personal contact or may be confined purely to the page, as in the instance of Goethe's love for the poetry of Hafiz or Schami's appreciation of Goethe. It is the engagement of the mind and emotions across geographical and historical distances that matter, together with the language in which that engagement is expressed. The extra dimension of an outsider's or newcomer's perspective can, in the right hands, make an original contribution to the best literature for children wherever they live, since children – as Sultan Hakim believed – can only benefit from the often serendipitous connections which produce such stories and poetry. Who, for example, could have foreseen a line through time and space joining a medieval Persian poet, a German genius of the eighteenth and nineteenth centuries, and two contemporary children's authors, one of them a Syrian writing in German – a constellation which currently hovers in the minds of a number of young German readers?

1   In a conversation with Goethe recorded by his friend Eckermann in 1827 (see Schamil and Gutschhahn, 1999, pp.70-71)

Children's Books referred to

Hiçilmaz, G (1993) *The Frozen Waterfall*, London: Faber and Faber.

Lingard, J (1989) *Tug of War*, London: Hamish Hamilton.

Lingard, J (1991). *Between Two Worlds*, London: Hamish Hamilton.

O'Sullivan, E. and Rösler, D. (1983). *I like you – und du?* Frankfurt: Fischer.

Schami, R. and Knorr, P. (1990). *Der Wunderkasten*, Weinheim: Beltz.

Schami, A. (1991). *A Handful of Stars*. Tr. Rika Lesser, London: Penguin.

Schami, R. (1996). *Hürdenlauf oder Von den unglaublichen Abenteuern, die emer erlebt der seThe Geschichte zu Ende erzählen will,* Frankfurt: Institut für Jugendbuchforschung der Johann Wolfgang Goethe-Universität.

Schami, R. and Gutzschhahn, U. (1999). Der geheime Bericht über den Dichter Goethe, Munich: Hanser.

*   Note: with the exception of *A Handful of Stars,* which has been published in English, translations from the German of the titles of Rafik Schami's books and extracts are my own.

Alice in different Wonderlands: Varying approaches in the German translations of an English children's classic

Emer O'Sullivan

Die Jhr deutsche Kinder seid	(German children,
heißt wilkommen diese Maid!	Welcome this maiden!
Aufenthaltserlaubnisscheine	She doesn't (to my knowledge)
hat sie, meines Wissens, keine;	Have a residence permit.
doch ein Büchlein – eins mit Bildern –	But she has brought along a book,
bringt sie mit: das mag sie schildern	One with pictures, which will describe her
besser als ein Paß es kann.	Better than any passport.
Lest es durch und sagt mir dann,	Read it and then tell me
ob das Kind nicht unter Euch	Whether this child may stay with you
bleiben soll im Deutschen Reich.	In the German Empire.
Sagen laßt mich noch das eine:	And one other thing:
Gebt Ihr Geld aus für die Kleine,	If you have paid for her
gibt auch sie den Reingewinn	She will donate the profit
der 'Deutschen Kinderhilfe' hint	To the German Children's Charity.)[1]
(Carroll, 1922)	

The maiden thus presented to German children in 1922 by the translator Robert Guy Lionel Barrett isn't German by birth, otherwise she would need neither a residence permit nor a passport, but she does speak perfect German. When she is taken by surprise and utters sentences which aren't linguistically correct, we are told: 'sie war so bestürzt, daß sie ganz vergaß, richtig deutsch zu sprechen' (Carroll, 1922,12) (she was so dismayed that she forgot how to speak proper German). Lewis Carroll's Alice – for it is she – is transformed from a Victorian English girl to a German *Mädchen* in many German translations of the famous novel.

Shortly after *Alice's Adventures in Wonderland* was published by Macmillan in 1865, Charles Dodgson started to examine the possibility of having the book translated into French and German. Letters to his publisher reveal that he even did some market research to see if it would be well received abroad[2]. Having clear ideas about how the book should be translated, preferably by 'someone who had written something of the sort, so as to have some sort of sympathy with the style: if possible, someone who writes verses' (quoted in Weaver, 1964,33), he went about finding the French and German translators himself. Antoine Zimmermann, a German teacher living in England at the time and known to Dodgson's aunt, produced the first German translation, closely monitored by Dodgson (who, incidentally, didn't speak the language). On the 4th September 1868 he wrote in his diary: 'Had two hours with Miss Zimmermann, looking over her German version of *Alice*' (Green, 1953, Vol 2: 274). Published in 1869, it was the first translation of the complete *Alice in Wonderland.*

Since then over thirty different German translations have been published (not counting abridged versions and translations into other media)[3]. Can *Alice in Wonderland* be successfully translated into German or, for that matter, into any other language? Dodgson's friends certainly didn't think so at the time. In a letter to Macmillan he wrote: 'Friends here seem to think that the book is untranslatable into either French or German, the puns and songs being the chief obstacles' (quoted in Weaver 1964, 33). Word play on the highest level, linguistic jokes which can't be translated easily, poems, parodies; the English language not only provides the context for much of his humour, it itself is frequently its very object. "Mine is a long and sad tale!' (...) 'It is a long tail, certainly (...), but why do you call it sad?" The chance of there being a homophone in any other language which denotes both a story and the flexible prolongation of an animal's spine is slim. And what about: 'But they were in the well' (...) 'Of course they were, (...), well in.'? When we bear in mind that German is generally not as rich in homophones as English and that there is no great tradition of punning in German literature, the challenge facing translators is more than apparent.

Surprisingly, however, challenges to translators can also be found where English readers would least suspect them. 'Alice was beginning to get very tired of sitting by her sister on the bank', the opening words of the novel, were translated in 1912 by the second German translator, Helene Scheu-Riesz, as follows: 'Alice fing gerade an, es sehr langweilig zu finden, daß sie da neben ihrer Schwester auf der Bank saß' (Carroll, 1912, 5). The English and German words 'Bank' aren't equivalents but so-called 'false friends'. Apart from the financial institution, German 'Bank' also denotes 'bench'. Thus the translation reads: Alice was beginning to get very tired of sitting by her sister on the bench. The illustration by Frans Haacken in Figure 1 shows

Figure 1: From Carroll 1967: Alice sitting on a bench.

Alice sitting on a bench, a mistake which can be found in over half of all German translations between 1912 and the present.

Alice in Wonderland is full of explicit and implicit cultural references which present German translators with further difficulties. These include topographical elements ('Wherever you go to on the English coast you find a number of bathing machines in the sea'), eating habits ('hot buttered toast'), references to historical or cultural figures (William the Conquerer, Shakespeare), regional and social accents (the Gryphon's Cockney, Pat's Irish accent), currency (pounds, shillings, pence), weights and measures (inches, feet; ounces, pounds) and names. They are the aspects which make a text – at least superficially – recognisably foreign, and are those which are most readily changed, especially in the translation of children's literature. They were 'foreign' to the young German reader in 1869, even if becoming increasing less so in the latter half of the 20th century. The names of some of the characters in *Alice in Wonderland* can't be transferred easily into another language because they are personifications of sayings or figures from English nursery rhymes – the Mad Hatter, the March Hare, the Cheshire Cat, the Queen of Hearts and her court.

But beyond these – admittedly difficult – linguistic and cultural elements lies a more fundamental issue which had to be addressed by each of the thirty and more translators of *Alice in Wonderland:* how can you translate a book which is so totally unlike anything produced by German authors for children? How do you deal with its dream-like quality, its perverted logic, its incomprehensibility? Is the book suitable for children, is it acceptable for German children? Each German translation of *Alice in Wonderland* can be read as an answer to these questions; an answer provided by the individual translator and influenced by predominant concepts of childhood and attitudes towards what constituted children's literature in Germany at the time of each particular translation.

The translations range from those which infantilize the novel to others which offer an exclusively adult reading of it. It is presumptuous to offer a simple classification of 130 years of translation history which has produced over 30 different versions of the same book but, for the sake of a brief overview, it is nonetheless possible to identify four main approaches:

- the fairy-tale approach

- the explanatory approach

- the literary approach and

- the approach which is both literary and accessible to children.

The fairy-tale approach
Nonsense was a genre more or less alien to mainstream German literature until the 1960s. Individual writers had written in a similar mode prior to that – Christian Morgenstern[4], Joachim Ringelnatz or members of the Dada movement such as Hans Arp or Kurt Schwitters being prime examples – but their work didn't enjoy widespread popularity. Nonsense in children's literature was unheard of. To make *Alice in Wonderland* accessible to young German readers and straightforward for themselves, translators looked to the home-grown product which resembled it most, the fairytale. The fairy-tale mood is introduced in paratexts about the author Lewis Carroll who, according to Karl Köstlin, told the Liddell sisters the story of Alice's adventures in his room 'an den langen Winterabenden' (during the long winter evenings) (Köstlin, 1949). In Franz Sester's translation the point of the 'dry story' is missed entirely as it is replaced by the story of Little Red Riding Hood (*Rotkäppchen* in German). An obvious adaptation of *Alice in Wonderland* to the fairy-tale model can be seen in R.G. L. Barrett's translation (Carroll, 1922). In it, the 'Mad Tea Party' is transformed into a German coffee circle with figures which look as if they have just emerged from the German fairy-

tale forest. Instead of the Mad Hatter and the March Hare, we find the cobbler 'Meister Pechfaden' and the 'Osterhase', the Easter Bunny. Barrett's translation was reissued, barely changed, by the translator Walther Günther Schreckenbach in 1949, illustrated by Hanne Umrain-Fischer. Her picture of the 'Mad Tea Party' scene in figure 2 shows the social gathering seated in front of a fairy-tale Easter Bunny house with Alice, her blonde hair in plaits, the cobbler broad and bearded, and the Easter Bunny wearing homely slippers which can be seen under a tablecloth bordered with little hearts. A wonderland, as one commentator remarked, in which the seven dwarfs would also feel at home (cf. Aljonka, 1987,18). Not a trace is there of the danger which laces the scene in the original, not a hint of the mad unpredictability of the characters; eradicated, too, is the comic element, the drollness of the situation.

The explanatory approach

Many German translations try to turn *Alice in Wonderland* into a comprehensible book, to explain away the inexplicable. In them, language as meaningful communication is no longer questioned or undermined. The disturbing, grotesque, threatening dimension of Lewis Carroll's book is eliminated. When the White Rabbit asks Pat where he is, the gardener replies: 'Sure then I'm here! Digging for apples, yer honour.' The Rabbit responds to this bit of nonsense with his angry 'Digging for apples, indeed!', but this alone wasn't enough, in the opinion of the translator Liselotte Remané, to lessen the confusion caused by Pat's remark. Hence the gardener in her version is more 'sensibly' 'Beim Kartoffelbuddeln', digging for potatoes (1967 translation).

One of the most extreme examples of extensive explanation occurs in Franz Sester's translation of 1948, in the passage where the 'Mock Turtle' is first mentioned. He is introduced as follows in the original:

> 'Then the Queen left off, quite out of breath, and said to Alice, 'Have you seen the Mock Turtle yet?'

> 'No', said Alice. 'I don't even know what a Mock Turtle is.'

> 'It's the thing Mock Turtle Soup is made from,' said the Queen. 'I never saw one, or heard of one.'

> 'Come on, then', said the Queen, 'and he shall tell you his history.'

Franz Sester obviously found this somewhat unsatisfactory. What were his young readers supposed to think a Mock Turtle was? He therefore added, directly after the Queen tells Alice to follow her, a lengthy passage which has no equivalent in the English original. In it we find a culturally adapted Alice;

Figure 2: From Carroll 1949: Alice in a German fairy-tale forest.

she is a well-behaved, somewhat boring English-learning German schoolgirl. In the course of the explanation of what a Mock Turtle is, the reader is introduced to Alice's teacher and Alice's aunt and is also given a recipe for Mock Turtle soup:

> 'Wie kann man mich zu einem Tier flihren', so dachte Alice, 'das es doch gar nicht gibt?' Alice hatte schon im zweiten Jahre Englisch. Die Lehrerin hatte den Kindern bereits beigebracht, daß 'turtle' auf deutsch 'Schildkröte' bedeutet, während 'mock' auf deutsch 'nachgemacht' heißt. Mock-Turtle-Suppe war also nichts anderes als eine 'nachgemachte' Schildkrötensuppe, die gar nicht mit Schildkrötenfleisch zubereitet war. Die Folge des guten englischen Unterrichts, den die Lehrerin gab, war also, daß alle Mädchen der Quinta genau wußten, was eine Mock Turtle war und aus Dankbarkeit der Lehrerin gleich den schönen Spitznamen 'Die Mockturtle' gaben.
>
> Bei der Hochzeit ihrer Tante hatte Alice auch einmal in der Küche zugesehen, wie die Mock-Turtle-Suppe zubereitet wurde. Sie erinnerte sich noch genau, daß in die Suppe em halber Kalbskopf, ein Ochsengaumen, Suppengrun und andere Zutaten kamen. Später bei Tisch hatten der klemen Alice die Kalbskopf- und Ochsengaumenwürfelchen in der Suppe besonders gut geschmeckt, denn, wißt ihr, weun es sich urn Essen handelte, hatte Alice immer ein besonders großes Interesse und ein ausgezeichnetes Gedächtnis. So etwas behielt sie immer viel besser als englische oder französische Vokabeln.' (Carroll, 1949,69)

> ('How can I be brought to an animal which doesn't even exist?', thought Alice. This was Alice's second year learning English in school. The teacher had already told the children that 'turtle' was 'Schildkröte' in German and that 'mock' meant 'nachgemacht'. So Mock Turtle Soup was nothing other than an imitation turtle soup which wasn't made with turtle meat at all. Thanks to the excellent English instruction by their teacher, each girl in the 6th class knew exactly what a Mock Turtle was, and out of gratitude to their teacher they gave her the lovely nickname 'the Mock Turtle'.
>
> At her aunt's wedding Alice had also seen in the kitchen how Mock-Turtle-Suppe was made. She could remember exactly that half a calf's head, an ox's' gum, some carrots, onion, celery, leeks and parsley and other ingredients were used to make the soup. Later, during the meal, little Alice especially savoured the small pieces of calf s head and ox's gum in the soup because, you know, when it came to eating, Alice was always very interested and remembered anything to do with it much better than English or French vocabulary.)

In an attempt to make the unfamiliar more familiar, Sester misses the point of the book and produces a nanny translation devoid of any nonsense. Any incidental humourous effect is involuntarily.

The literary approach

A watershed in the history of the German reception of *Alice in Wonderland* occurred in 1963, when both *Alice* books were translated by Christian Enzensberger. It was a period in German literature which witnessed a sudden interest in nonsense and the absurd – anthologies of nonsense poetry started to appear in the mid-1960s, German pioneers such as Morgenstern and Schwitters were rediscovered, contemporary authors like H.C. Artmann and Ernst Jandl celebrated; the first German translation of some of Edward Lear's limericks appeared in 1964, over a hundred years after they were published in England. With Enzensberger's intelligent and creative translation of *Alice in Wonderland,* German readers could finally get an inkling of the complexity and brilliance of Carroll's original. Translation is always primarily an individual act of reception and interpretation of an original text by the translator; in an Afterword, Enzensberger tells his readers what 'his' *Alice in Wonderland* is about: it reflects the state of modern man in a cruel, Kafkaesque world devoid of sense. To underline the apparently universal applicability of Carroll's vision Enzensberger, while recognising the specifically English origin of the books, elected not to literally translate references to England, preferring instead to substitute south German lords for the Earls of Mercia and Northumbria and Napoleon for William the Conqueror, Goethe for Shakespeare and so on.

On the other hand he gives a literal translation of Carroll's parodies rather than attempting to parody German poems. 'How doth the little crocodile' is translated as a parody of Isaac Watts' 'How doth the little busy bee', with Enzensberger using the same key lexical elements, the same metre, the same strategies as Carroll did to satirise empty moralising by retaining the danger of the crocodile under his seemingly friendly exterior. It is, therefore, a perfect German parody of an English poem. Only a reader familiar with Watts' original verses can fully get the joke. While making the geographical reference universal by localising the story in Germany on the one hand, he elects, on the other, to retain the temporal distance between the novel of 1865 and readers of the 1960s and produces a text which has a distinct 19th century feel to it. With its odd archaic turns of phrase in German and its opaque references, Enzensberger's translation is that of the classical text which *Alice in Wonderland* has become, complete with the patina lent by time and acclaim. Thus it is a translation for adults, for intellectuals even which, in contrast to Lewis Carroll's original, loses sight of the child reader. It reproduces an almost exclusively adult reading of the text.

The approach which is both literary and accessible to children

Alice in Wonderland is a text with dual address. It can be read with pleasure by both child and adult readers, the adults being attracted by the complex games played with language and reason and the' psychological depth. But it is not a book primarily addressed to adults. As Barbara Wall rightly claims:

> Dodgson began with his narrator's voice confidentially addressing a known and loved narratee, and he sustained this manner to the end. In the tone of the narrator's voice we can constantly hear the desire to please and to gain the respect of the Alice-narratee. Dodgson, in this way, broke new ground: he put his narratee, and hence his child audience, first, and showed how it was possible both to address children unselfconsciously, not caring if other adults overheard, and to share a story with them. (Wall, 1991,109f)

His single address to children became dual address without ever losing sight of the child audience. The child was not the addressee of Enzensberger's translation, but his 'literary' translation revealed to German speakers the complexity and quality of a book hitherto dumbed down by most of the translations which, with a clear child reader in mind (and one who couldn't cope with a challenge), held no attraction for the adult reader. This changed in the 1980s, thanks partly to Enzensberger having shown what *Alice* was made of and partly due to changes in German children's literature, which, for various reasons, was becoming more open to hitherto unknown or unaccepted forms of humour and nonsense.

A small number of translations published in the late 1980s and early 1990s with varying degrees of success in terms of literary quality – some with funnier and more intelligent word games and parodies than the others – have one thing in common: they are to be enjoyed and understood by children but are not prepared to compromise the quality and the spirit of the original. Barbara Teutsch, one of the translators, indirectly criticised Enzensberger's translation when she spoke, in an afterword, about her translation: even the most ambiguous of jokes in Carroll's original were for children and not for linguistic *highbrows*, she said (using the English word). She wanted to try to position Carroll's fun where it could be enjoyed by children of today (cf. Teutsch, 1989, 141). The translators achieve this goal through their creative use of language and by neutralising (but not falsifying) the historical and, in some cases, the cultural context. The historical dimension of the novel, so central to Enzensberger's version, is not emphasised in these translations. The language is contemporary but not faddish, Carroll's parodies are replaced by parodies of well-known German poems. One of the most successful of these, by Siv Bublitz, is her 'translation' of 'How doth the little crocodile'. It is a parody of Goethe's famous poem 'Der Fischer' (The Fisherman), dynamic and cheeky in its diction but nonetheless it manages to retain the smiling and murderous crocodile:

Das Wasser rauscht, das Wasser tost,	(The waters sweep, the waters swell,
em Krokodil sitzt drin,	A crocodile therein
sieht nach dem kleinen Fischerboot	Looks at the little fishing boat
und grinst so vor sich hin.	And to himself does grin
Daun schnappt es zu, das geht ruck, zuck,	Then jaws snap shut all in a flash
da ist der Fischer weg;	O fisherman, adieu!
das Krokodil hat Magendruck,	The crocodile has tummy ache
das Boot, es hat em Leck.	The boat is leaking, too.)[5]
(Carroll, 1993: 23)	

The translations which are both literary and accessible can also be read with enjoyment by adults, thus reproducing, perhaps most faithfully, the dual address of the original.

The approaches described here – the fairy-tale, the explanatory, the literary approach and the one which is both literary and accessible to children – cannot be seen as strictly chronological progressions. Enzensberger's translation was without doubt in part responsible for the superior quality of the later translations, but, since it appeared in 1963, further translation with 'nanny' or dumbing-down tendencies have been issued for children. Nonetheless a certain historical progression cannot be denied, with current translational norms demanding higher standards of literary translations for children.

In his influential book *Les livres, les enfants et les hommes,* published in 1932, the French comparative literary scholar Paul Hazard created the idea of a 'world republic of childhood' in which children of all nations read the children's books of all nations.

The 'world republic of childhood' as Hazard called it knows no borders, no foreign languages: 'Smilingly the pleasant books of childhood cross all the frontiers; there is no duty to be paid on inspiration' (Hazard, 1944,147). Even today, children's literature – especially its classics – is frequently regarded and referred to as the product of an international culture of childhood, monolingual, monocultural, in which international understanding is the order of the day. To speak in this nice, rather cosy and certainly very idealistic way about children's literature is to ignore both the conditions influencing its production and those underlining its cultural transfer. An inevitable consequence of these conditions is that the works change considerably in the course of time and on their ways across linguistic and cultural frontiers.

German books with the title *Alice im Wunderland* cannot, for the most part, be equated with Lewis Carroll's *Alice in Wonderland*. Most Germans today know *Alice in Wonderland* mainly thanks to Walt Disney. Compared to its reception in England and in other countries, Lewis Carroll's book simply wasn't a success in Germany, for which the poor quality of many of the thirty-one translations issued in the course of 130 years is partially responsible. The translations themselves are clear indicators of how translators and publishers felt such an excitingly innovative but also puzzling book should be presented to young German readers.

Notes
1. All translations of the German passages into English are by the author of this piece.
2. I am strongly advised to try a translation of 'Alice' into French, on the ground that French children are not nearly so well off for well illustrated books as English or German.' (quoted in Weaver, 1964, 33).
3. A comprehensive analysis as well as a bibliography of all the translations can be found in O'Sullivan (at press).
4. An excellent English translation of a selection of Morgenstern's poems by Anthea Bell can be found in: Christian Morgenstern: *Lullabies, Lyrics and Gallows Songs.* Selected and illustrated by Lisbeth Zwerger. Translated by Anthea Bell. North-South Books, 1995.
5. A special thanks to my sister, Maeve, for the enjoyable joint effort on this translation.

Translation of Alice in Wonderland

1869   Zimmerman, A., mit tweiundvierzig illustrationem von John Tenniel, Autorisierte Ausgabe. Leipzig, Hartknoch

1912   Scheu-Riesz, H. illust. Arthur Rackman. Weimar, Kiepenhauer

1922   Barrett, R.G.L. Illust. F.W. Roth. Selbstverlag des Ubersetzers, Nurnberg: Der Bund (in Komm)

1948   Schreckenbach, W.G. illust. Hanne Umrain Fischer. Numberg

1949   Sester, F. illust. Charlotte Strech-Ballot, Dusseldorf

1950   Kostlin, K. illust. Lilo Rasch-Nagele, Stuttgart Riederer

1953   Green, R.L. (ed) The Diaries of Lewis Carroll. London, Cassell

1963   Ensensberger, C., mit siebenundreissig. illust. des Autors, Frankfurt, Insel

1967   Retrane, L., mit Nachdichtungen von Martin Remnne; illust. F. Haacken, Berlin, Holz

1985   von Cube, N. Illust. Siggi Grunow; mit einem Nachwort von Roger Willemsen und ein Anmerkung zur Ubersetzung von N. von Cube. Munich, Boer

1987   Aljonka, A.I. edited by the British Council, Munich and the International Youth Library, Munich

1989   Teutsch, B. illust. J. Tenniel. Hamburg, Dressler

1993   Aubliitz, S. mit Bildern von Klaus Einsikat. Nachwort von D.E. Zimmer, Reinstek, Rotfuchs

1998   Jászó, A. The magician strategy in Hungary. In *The Moonmins in the World – learning with text.* ed. K. Sarnavouri, Turku, University of Turku

Children's Literature and International Identity?
A Translator's Viewpoint

Anthea Bell

From where the translator working out of other European languages into English stands, it would be good to see a little more sense of international identity in the approach of the book trade to European children's books. When I became a translator in the 1960s (by chance, as one did then) it happened, also by chance, to be in the field of children's literature. To this day I have a great fondness for Otfried Preussler's first children's book, his fantasy *Der Kleine Wassermann*, which as *The Little Water-Sprite* was my own first translation. I was what the translating profession calls a kitchen-table translator, a rather disparaging term suggesting the amateurish approach of a part-timer, but it applied to me quite literally while I worked on my kitchen table with a usually tolerant baby in a carry-cot beside me. Even at that time, the number of children's books translated into English from other languages was far smaller than the number of English children's books accepted for publication in other European countries. But it wasn't infinitesimal. When the *Times Literary Supplement* published its twice-yearly children's supplements of those days, a fair number of foreign books featured in the reviews. When the St. James Press published the first edition of its *Twentieth-Century Children's Writers,* and I contributed a survey of foreign children's writers who had been translated into English, there was something to survey – not just from the earlier years of the century, but right up to the publication of that first edition in the 1970s.

However, when I was asked to revise the article for the second and then the third editions, it turned out that there was very little new material to be added. And at the time of the fourth edition, published in 1995, the number of translations had fallen to a level where a new revision of that particular article was not thought necessary. Most foreign books that actually had been recently published in English were picture-books – which continues, for fairly obvious reasons, to be the case. Artwork appeals across language barriers.

None the less, it is intriguing to notice what a difference artwork can in fact make to the national or international identity of a story-book. The winner of the 1999 Marsh Award for Children's Literature in Translation was Patricia Crampton's translation of Gudrun Pausewang's moving Holocaust story, *The Final Journey*, which had no illustrations. But the artwork was prominent in the close runner-up, Jostein Gaarder's *Hello? Is Anybody There?* (Orion Children's Books, translated by James Anderson in a version highly commended by the jury panel). The original Norwegian illustrations had not been used for the English edition, and it was fascinating to see how the new artwork by Sally Gardner made the book almost a double translation, of both text and pictures. Both sets of illustrations were excellent, but they were in very different styles: the original Norwegian pictures made the extra-terrestrial who visits earth and discusses its phenomena with the child narrator distinctly more weird and way-out than he appears in the new pictures for the English-speaking world, which have a nostalgic charm about them.

The usual reason given for the disproportion, both now and in the past, between children's books translated into and out of English is the existence of the very flourishing tradition of English children's literature. It's a good point, but not really a justification for ignoring the best of the foreign equivalents. And even with that tradition of acknowledged and continuing excellence behind it, children's literature in the United Kingdom is in something of a ghetto. Literary ghettos do exist: in the English-speaking world children's books are in one and translation in general is in another, so it is hardly surprising that translations of children's literature are consigned to the ghetto twice over.

In support of the first part of that contention, I think I need only say that at the time of writing – the summer of 1999 – all the fiction best-seller lists in the United Kingdom are headed by a children's book: J.K. Rowling's third Harry Potter story. Or they would be, if outraged cries of, 'Unfair!' had not been raised by the publishers of the adult novels which would occupy that position but for Harry Potter. The general idea is that he and his creator should stay in the ghetto where they belong, featuring only on the lists of best-selling children's books. Well, it looks to me perfectly fair, and it is entertaining to see a children's book taking on the big guns and winning. Some years ago one of the national broadsheets ran its annual comment on the most-borrowed-books from UK public libraries, courtesy of the figures issued by the Public Lending Right office (which in fact provides separate sets of such figures for both adult and children's books). The newspaper commented that many of the most-borrowed novels were genre fiction – 'children's books, romance and Westerns' implying that they therefore hardly counted for the purposes of the survey. What, I thought, *all* children's books, from Enid Blyton to Leon Garfield and Anne Fine, all simply lumped together as genre fiction? I was going to write to the paper and say so; better still, since translators don't have a high profile, I was going to ask a couple of distinguished children's authors to do so instead. I refrained only because the Gulf War began next day, so obviously no one was likely to take any notice. All the same, children are the adults of the future, and the books they read in childhood help to form their minds; neither they nor the books written for them deserve wholesale dismissal. I'm reminded of the television transmission of the Booker Prize ceremony in the year when Jill Paton Walsh's complex and fine novel of ideas *Knowledge of Angels* very nearly won, and when one of the TV pundits discussing the entries commented that she was 'a children's writer', suggesting that her earlier children's books somehow disqualified her present, adult work from being considered along with the other five contenders at all.

As for the ghetto in which translated works in general reside in English-language publishing – perhaps it is symptomatic of our inborn British insularity that one journalist, writing of Goethe in the great man's centenary year of 1999, patronisingly described him as a 'near-genius'. Presumably only a true Brit deserves the accolade of recognition as an outright genius. However, taking a longer view, I suppose most reasonably well-educated people, if asked for their personal lists of the great literary works of the world, would automatically include a number of authors some at least of whom would have to be read in translation. Everyone's list would vary, of course, but one might expect the frequent occurrence of such names as those of Homer, Cervantes, Rabelais, Dante, Shakespeare, Pushkin, Goethe, Corneille, Racine and Moliére, Victor Hugo, Flaubert, Dostoevsky and Tolstoy, Proust, Chekhov – not to mention the Bible.

Many if not all of the works of these writers would have been read in translation by the compilers of such lists; one could say that translators are actually necessary to help supply the furnishings of a well-stocked mind, even though translators themselves seldom like reading translations. (My own great regret is my inability to read the major works of Russian literature in the original.) They thereby, inadvertently, qualify themselves to become translators, being determined to acquire the skill of reading books in other languages as soon as possible. This is one of the ironies of the job. As I mentioned above, it's a low-profile profession, and I really think it should be: after all, if you have done your job properly as a translator then readers will not notice that the words on the page are actually your words. You interpret your author in much the same way as an actor interprets a play, but with less leeway for freedom of interpretation because your duty is to the author and not your own ego. But if there is any clumsiness, if translationese sets in, of course reviewers will pounce, and quite right too. I have heard it argued publicly that all translation is a bad thing just because it's not the original – still, if translators are an evil I do think we are probably a necessary evil.

I would go on to suggest that the internationally well-stocked mind postulated above will have acquired the habit of reading while young, finding in books an enrichment of life, or sometimes an escape route, and that to prepare it to select the great names of world literature automatically for its list, it should have had not just the best works of children's literature in English but their counterparts from other languages made available in childhood.

Very few English children are bilingual; apart from that tiny minority even the linguistically talented, those who pick up the basics of another language quickly, will not usually be able to read children's books in that language while they are still the ideal age for them. I have a favourite quotation from Dr Johnson, who commented, 'I am always for getting a boy forward in his learning; for that is a sure good. I would let him at first read any English book which happens to engage his attention; because you have done a great deal when you have brought him to have entertainment from a book. He'll get better books afterwards.' By 'better books', Johnson probably meant those works of Greek and Latin literature with which an educated person of his time would have been familiar. The modern equivalent might be an acquaintance with the great works of literature written over, say, the last thousand years in modern European languages. This is the area where I see a specific part being played by translations and translators in general, and by translations and translators of children's literature in particular, preparing the ground for a more international outlook.

(In parenthesis, the patronising attitude often adopted to children's writers that I mentioned above applies in spades to the translators of children's books. In general people assume that the vocabulary of such books is simple, and the task is therefore extremely easy. As a matter of fact, that is not so. Even in a picture book – perhaps especially in a picture book – every word counts and must be carefully evaluated. I was once asked to edit a translation of a collection of little stories for young children done by a noted scientific and legal translator who had expressed a wish to translate a children's book for a change. Whatever his abilities in the fields of science and the law, as a translation for children it was useless. A salvage operation was required rather than straightforward editing – and all translators know how tricky it is to work on someone else's translation; far easier to start from scratch.)

There is no shortage, I'm happy to say, of good translations of children's books *from* English. There is definitely a shortage of good translations *into* English. In 1996, at a seminar organised by the Institut fur Jugendbuchforschung of the Johann Wolfgang Goethe University of Frankfurt to discuss the state of German-language children's literature internationally, I found that the participants from Germany, Austria and Switzerland were well aware of the disproportion. From all that was said, one concluded that publishers and authors in the German-speaking countries had just about given up on the English language market for children's books, while conversely so many titles are translated into German that publishers' lists scrupulously distinguish between those translated 'from the English', 'from the American', 'from the Australian', and so forth. As British delegate to the seminar, I felt apologetic on behalf of the UK. It was and still is my impression, based partly on those lists I have seen of entries for the Mildred L. Batchelder prize for a translated children's book in the USA, that the situation in North America is slightly better, although Jeffrey Garrett, the American delegate at the same seminar, was not so sure. And Dr Ronald Jobe of Vancouver tells me that 'there certainly are more translated titles available, but I wonder if they are any more successful [than in the UK]. A lot of it is due to lack of promotion and publicity.' The double ghetto again, I suspect.

Translators alone cannot supply the English-speaking world with those works of good European children's literature I have in mind. Publishers are involved, and of course publishers are not charities. It is easy to understand why they hesitate to risk accepting a foreign book and then going to the expense of translation, not to mention promotion and publicity. On the whole, we are monoglots in the UK – a little school French may linger on, although notoriously the French and the English spend six years allegedly learning each other's language at school, and usually still can't conduct a proper conversation at the end of that time. (It's arguable that French should not be the first modern language taught. Other Germanic languages are more like English, and many say that among the Romance languages, Spanish is more easily learnt from scratch than French.) Naturally, a publisher who can't read a book for himself and must rely on readers' reports will have to know and trust those readers to a high degree, and will be wary of investing money in buying rights and commissioning translations.

It can be worth it, however. Take the interesting case of the strip cartoon, a textual and artistic genre very much in its own right on the Continent, particularly France, where whole seminars, magazines and fan clubs are devoted to the *bande dessinée*. Of all the many French and Belgian series, only *Tintin* and *Astérix* have sold well and have become thoroughly acclimatised on the

English market, for different but perfectly comprehensible reasons. Tintin is a hero very much in the plucky British boy-scout mould of the time of his first appearance (I believe some minor revision has been carried out later in the light of changing modern attitudes). There is nostalgia involved, of the cracking good yarn type. And Astérix appeals to that British sense of humour which likes to laugh at the noble stuffed shirts of history, enjoys anachronism, and shares a taste for puns and wordplay with our French neighbours. Moreover, inherent in the strip cartoon form itself is an element of subversion and mild anarchy, a healthy spirit of contradiction challenging pious commonplaces, political correctness and the Establishment. These characteristics, in my view, make Tintin and Astérix such good examples of their kind that they have been successful in the United Kingdom. I have read my way, however, through towering piles of other *bande dessinée* series, tales ranging from deranged science fiction through downright pornography to the nauseatingly twee, because French publishers cannot understand why, if Tintin and Astérix are acceptable, UK publishers can't sell other works in the genre.

None the less, Astérix should be an encouragement to publishers, for in the 1960s, when he had been going strong for some years in France, a number of British publishing houses turned him down on the grounds that he was too Gallic to cross the Channel, and were proved wrong. I have always thought the character is not just French but genuinely European, and that accounts for his success outside France. He is hugely popular, for instance, in Germany, the Netherlands and Scandinavia. (An eminent Slavonic scholar said to me recently that he could not see the series appealing in Russia and other points east, that it was inconceivable for the Slavs to laugh at their proud past history in the same way as the French, the English and other Western Europeans, but after I had quoted his views in print I had a charming letter from an Astérix follower, obviously of wide linguistic talents and interests, disagreeing and citing a number of comic Russian writers in refutal.)

Having been involved, with my colleague Derek Hockridge, in the English translations of these stories ever since Hodder & Stoughton decided to take the risky plunge into the uncertain waters of the Channel between Gaul and Britain, I have been intrigued to discover that children and even adults who read the English versions do not always realise that they were first written in French. I corresponded recently with a student at Heidelberg, Christa Claussen, whose lively and very readable thesis for her diploma in translation and interpreting was a comparative study of the entire Astérix saga in the original French and its German, English, Italian and Catalan translations. I was intrigued by her conclusion that the German and English translations, just *because* they had to approach the originals at more of a tangent than the

Romance languages, had on the whole been more successful in rendering the humour. This was a case where – in only apparent contradiction to my comment above about the translator's obligation to the author – great freedom in the translation of the original was the best way of remaining faithful to its spirit.

And I see other areas where there are parallels, at the turn of the century, between British and Continental publishing for children. The novel that hovers on the line between the mainstream adult and the children's markets is a familiar phenomenon in the German-speaking world. In 1997 I read a remarkable book by Reinhard Kaiser, *Königskinder*, the real-life 1930s letters of a young man of Jewish descent to his Swedish girlfriend, picked up by chance at a stamp auction by the author, who then managed to trace the subsequent history of the ill-fated couple. The book is fact, not fiction, although it becomes a fascinating tale of literary detection, and I read it as an adult book, but I was glad and not at all surprised to hear that it had won the 1997 German Jugendbuchpreis. Hans Magnus Enzensberger's time-travel fantasy for older children, scheduled for English publication in the year 2000, is another example of a book on the borderline between the adult and children's markets, and shows a famous author quite clearly not writing down to children, but relishing the opportunities offered by his subject. Similarly, in the present flourishing state of native English-language children's literature, adults as well as children are appreciating new books on or close to that borderline by writers such as Anne Fine, Philip Pullman, Peter Dickinson, Jan Mark, David Almond, Melvin Burgess, Susan Price. Famously, the first of J.K. Rowling's Harry Potter books had to be provided with an alternative jacket for adults, so that they wouldn't be ashamed to be seen reading it, and the third of Philip Pullman's *His Dark Materials* trilogy is eagerly awaited at the time of writing; I'd guess that a number of purchasers will be adults buying for themselves before – or if – they hand the book on to children.

So I for one do see a welcome *rapprochement* between attitudes in the British and the Continental European markets for children's literature at the beginning of the new millennium. All is not doom and gloom. One of the books I was able to cover in that first *Twentieth-Century Children's Writers* article, Anne Holm's *I am David*, is about to be reissued by Egmont Children's Books in its forthcoming list of Mammoth Literature in Translation, to be launched in the year 2000. The idea is bold, and so is the title of the list. Back in the 1960s there was a whole list published by University of London Press devoted to nothing but prize-winning children's books from other languages in English translation. Here is a welcome recurrence of such an idea. The entrants for the 1999 Marsh Award, for which translations of books for children and young people published over the previous two years qualified, amounted to around seven, and that was regarded as a fairly good score. Since one hopes that the award will acquire the same status (and number of entries) as the Batchelder prize in the States, it is good to realise that qualifying entries for 2001 now projected or already in production may already outnumber the small but high-quality 1999 entry. For the first time in quite a number of years, the prospects for a more international attitude to children's literature in the English-speaking world begin look good.

Children's books referred to

Gaarder, Jostein, *Hello? Is Anybody There?* trs. James Anderson, Orion Children's Books, 1997

Holm, Anne, *I am David,* 1965

Kaiser, Reinhard, *Königskinder,* Schöffung & Co., 1996

Paton Walsh, Jill, *Knowledge of Angels,* Green Bay/Colt Books, 1994

Pausewang, Gudrun, *The Final Journey,* trs. Patricia Crampton, Viking, 1996

Preussler, Otfried: *The Little Water-Sprite,* trs. Anthea Bell, Abelard-Schuman Ltd., 1961

PART TWO
What Do We Tell Our Children?

History and their place in it come to children as family memories, local recollections, national and religious holidays and celebrations, as these join with folk legends and historical narratives in books to create specific views of 'the past'. The long time-line of recorded world history varies in tellings and transmissions as social groups distinguish themselves in terms of cultural conventions and affiliations. When children have sorted themselves out according to name, address, age and sex, they identify themselves tribally as belonging to a group with another name: Irish, Flemish, Magyar, African, West Indian, which accounts for other samenesses and differences, including skin colour and language. Primitive stereotypes of these distinctions penetrate deeply into children's self-awareness and linger long. In reading about past events. French visitors to London arrive at a station called Waterloo; British visitors to Paris are surprised to see, on public monuments, a list of British defeats at the hand of Napoleon carved on public monuments.

The emergence of stereotypes as ways of seeing other people is a complicated subject. History deals in oppositions and conflicts. The notion of tolerance is not older in written records than the seventeenth century. Happily, new perspectives, enlightened by studies of racism in children's books, now reject 'semantic stereotyping,' a description used by Anna Jászó, who, in the first of the papers in this section, shows just how difficult it is for authors and readers to overcome prejudice. Politicians may redraw boundaries, but they cannot enforce loyalties. Not even wars of 'liberation' can guarantee the abolition of crude judgements about national characteristics. The role of historical novels in the defining of Magyar history is a particularly interesting example.

When wars are a recent memory they are part of the oral tradition. Later, they are a serious, and not straightforward, topic for children's books. Where victory is the happy ending, many alternative accounts of the conflict may be ignored. During recent inter-continental research into the representations of war in books for children, Carol Fox discovered that 'literature is a major medium for nation defining'. Amongst the two hundred books in English devoted to twentieth century wars there are some classics which have already withstood the test of time, but in most children's books dealing with the second world war, there is 'a certain amount of nostalgia and myth-making'. Fox's conclusion, that reading about war in schools should be a 'multi-genre enterprise', is an idea that should be taken further, especially with regard to books for adults which older pupils are likely to read.

Francis Marcoin confronts the scene of modern literature for young people in France, where culture is an imperative political matter, and where new books, especially the *albums* (picture books in the UK), are enjoying a renaissance. He brings together the pride of an historical nation and its reliance for the upkeep of its place in the modern progressive world of industry and commerce on the people it once colonised and despised. In his examples, Serbo-Croat, Magrebin, Franco-Vietnamese, Algerian, Turkish, Greek and Chinese children go to school together. The authors revise the version of history that 'gave Gallic ancestors to all French children, even if they were black'. Marcoin is forthright in his belief that children's books are at the front line of this revolution.

FRIEND OR FOE?
Images of the Germans in Hungarian literature for young readers

Anna Adamik Jászó

Throughout the whole history of the human race there have been no questions which have caused more heartsearchings, tumults and devastation than the questions of the correspondence of words to facts. The mere mention of such words as 'religion', 'patriotism', and 'property' is sufficient to demonstrate this truth. Now, it is the investigation of the nature of the correspondence between word and fact, to use these terms in the widest sense, which is the proper and the highest problem of the science of meaning. (C.K. Ogden and I.A. Richards, 1923)

Nowadays, the examination of the differences in culture and peoples is an exciting one. Its most notable aspect is how we arrive at stereotypes, the semantic contents of simplified judgements that are brought about by either personal experience or cultural hearsay. It is enlightening as well as interesting to compare the opinion held by one group of people about another group: Hungarians' views of Germans, Russians or Ottomans, for example, or English notions about the French or Germans. It is particularly significant where different groups of peoples are represented in books for children and adolescents, where the beliefs, constructs and attitudes of the readers are still in the making.

This topic has a more extensive literature in multinational states like the UK and the USA than in Hungary, where it is a newer subject for discussion. (It is worth mentioning that Hungary became homogeneous after the Trianon Peace Treaty in 1920. During the Middle Ages and under the Hapsburgs, Hungary was a multinational country.) In Hungarian literature, a writer's description of Germans or Austrians, in historical fiction for example, depends on the prevailing view of these peoples at the time when the book is being written. Thus the reader encounters a threefold judgement: first, of the events at the time of their occurrence, next, the writer's view in his or her own time,

33

and then, the prevailing opinion about these past events when the reader reads about them. It is a complicated business to analyse historical fiction from one point of view, and, at the same time, to do justice to the 'otherness', not only of people and events, but also to the opinion one side held of the other. We need to know what stance the writer takes on events reported as 'facts', and how the writer's viewpoint is influenced by personal experience and the views of other writers.

Germans or Austrians (Hapsburgs) have always been present in Hungarian literature. Their shared history has left unpleasant associations in the minds of Hungarians. However, these antagonisms receded when older enmities gave way to more recent ones. Sometimes the German is the troublemaker, the intriguer. Often he is the foe, both cruel and wicked; at another time he is honest and worthy. He can be the ridiculous, comic enemy (as portrayed in folktales), but he can also be the generous friend, the protector even. In exceptional circumstances he is the partner, the companion.

General Considerations

Historical fiction establishes the idea of 'us and others', so I shall concentrate on examples written for readers between the ages of ten and sixteen for my discussion of national identity. I shall also include books written originally for adults but now favoured by the young. In Hungary the concept of children's literature differs from that more generally understood elsewhere. We include in this description adult books which became compulsory reading in both elementary and high schools.

Then, we must also take into consideration certain literary traditions involved in the characterisation of other nations, especially neighbouring ones. Ever since Herodotus we have inherited generalisations about the characteristics of different groups.. These are often over-simplified; the negative features especially are enlarged when poking fun at the characters in folklore. I think we should distinguish between objective characterisation and stereotypes, especially in literature of mediocre quality. In spite of the changes in awareness of cultural differences in the twentieth century, stereotypes and prejudices still flourish, probably because certain historical events were memorably cruel or provoked cruelty. During the first thousand years of our history, we lived together, literally, with the Austrians and the Germans, the two nations indistinguishable in this relationship in the early years. Later, the difference between them became clear. Thus, I should like to discuss (i) historical accounts, (ii) books about the 20th century, and then to try to construct educational implications.

Literary History: between the 9th and 19th centuries

Myths and legends became part of children's literature everywhere on a certain level of comprehensibility. The first narrative link between Hungarians and Germans is probably Krimhild or Ildiko, the widowed wife of Siegfried, the hero of the Nibelungenlied, who, after the death of her husband, became the wife of Attila, the King of the Huns, the Scourge of God, whose name does not sound nicely in the countries of Western Europe. Thus, Krimhild became part of the Hun-Hungarian mythology. (Note that there is no linguistic connection between the Huns of Turkish origin and the Hungarians of Finno-Ugric origin. According to the mythology recorded in mediaeval chronicles, the Huns and Hungarians have a common origin).

The greatest Hungarian poet, Janos Arany (1817-1882), reconstructed an epic from fragments around the figure of Krimhild, Attila and his brother, Buda. This poem, called *The Death of Buda,* was written in 1864. In it, Arany definitely encoded the ideas of the 1848-generation, according to which 'marriage with the Germans never leads to a happy end'. Here it is Krimhild who causes the conflict. More significant in this respect is another German, Dietrich of Bern (Detre the Saxon in Hungarian) who, cunning as a fox, hating the Huns, is the first German troublemaker in Hungarian literary history.

With regard to legends, three stories are worth mentioning. They are accounts of battles between Hungarians and Germans in the Middle Ages. The hero of the first is the Knight Andoras, the forefather of the Andrassi family, who, in a duel, defeated a knight much taller and stronger. After 896, when the Magyars came into the Carpathian Basin, they led several campaigns into Europe as it then was. Because of their appearance and military manner, these wild warriors were identified by the local inhabitants as returning Huns, which may have led to the false generic identification of the Huns as Hungarians. In 955, the Magyars were defeated at Augsburg by the river Lech. The leader of this last campaign was Lehel, the chieftain, who was famous for his splendid ornamental horn. After his defeat, the German Emperor, Konrad, wanted to execute him. Before the execution Lehel asked that he might blow his famous horn once more. He did so, then killed Konrad by knocking him on the head with the horn. According to popular belief, the dead Konrad served Lehel in the other world.

During the reign of the Arpad dynasty (1000-1301), the Germans attacked the Hungarian kingdom several times. Defeats and victories followed one another, but Hungary kept her independence, and even became a strong state of the same size and power as mediaeval England. Every Hungarian schoolchild is familiar with the brave deeds of Kund the Diver who sank the ship of the attacking Germans by causing leaks during a dark night at Pozsony (now

Bratislava), in 1052. It was Henry III who was forced to leave our country. We read his story in the novel by Laszlo Gereb, *Buvar Kund* (1951, and in the ballad by Mihaly Vorosmarty 1829). (The fictive account by Gereb is so good that I put it into my third grade reader.)

'Between two pagans and one homeland' is how a contemporary poem depicts the situation in Hungary after 1526. The two pagans are the enemies, the Ottomans and the Hapsburgs. After the occupation of the capital, Buda, by the Ottomans in1541, Hungary was divided into three parts; the middle one belonged to the Ottoman empire, the western part to the Hapsburg empire. Transylvania was relatively independent, paying taxes to the Sultan and suffering from the incursions of the Hapsburg mercenaries from time to time. This period lasted for 150 years. After the reoccupation of Buda in 1686, Hungary became part of the Hapsburg empire. 'Between the claws of the Eagle' – this line of a contemporary poem expresses our general feeling towards our western neighbour. The two-headed eagle appears on the coat of arms of the Hapsburgs.

Austrians and Germans are described in a whole series of historical fictions. One of our most famous writers, Geza Gardonyi (1863 – 1922) wrote the best historical fiction for children about the siege of the Eger – in Hungarian, *Egri csilagok;* in English, *The Eclipse of the Crescent Moon* (1901). It concentrates on the struggles of the Magyars against the Turks. The Hapsburgs had promised to help the defenders of the Eger, but the liberating army never arrived. So the Hungarians were left alone to defend their homeland and Christian Europe. The news of the victory quickly spread westward. Europe applauded and rejoiced. In Rome the Pope celebrated a mass of thanksgiving. The king was bombarded with letters of congratulation. It is not necessary to make a complicated content analysis in order to understand the following conversation, which occurs at the beginning of the novel between two old Magyars; their evaluation of the Austrians is clear.

> 'You'll serve as a hangman', screeched Cecey.
> 'And you as an Austrian', retorted the enraged priest.
> 'Hangman!'
> 'Austrian!'
> 'Dog-catcher!'
> 'Traitor!'
> By now the two old men were almost blue with rage as they roared at each other. Dobo waited for the moment when they could be dragged apart...
>
> 'So stop wrangling, for heaven's sake' he said uncomfortably, 'or rather, save that for the Turks'.

However, this is only one side of the coin. There were Austrians and Germans living among the Magyars as fellow-soldiers. One of the most pleasing episodes in the novel occurs when 'a fair, curly-haired' German artilleryman instructs the peasants how to load the cannons.

The 'between two pagans' situation is depicted in the story by Istvan Fekete (1900-1970) *The Last Will of the Aga of Koppany* (*A koppanyi testamentuma*, 1937). This is a favourite novel of Hungarian schoolchildren. It describes the situation in the second half of the 16th century, when either the Turkish soldiers or foreign mercenaries were in the border fortresses. There were often duels between Hungarians and Turks who in between times lived peacefully with each other. In an honest duel between Laszlo Babocsay and the Aga of Koppany, the young Hungarian kills the Turk. In his will, the Aga asks Laszlo to take his daughter and his money to Laszlo's mother. This is a difficult request as several years before, the Aga had killed Laszlo's father, also in a duel. But, finally, the mother accepts the little girl. The villain of the piece is Rudolf de Kales, a Vallon mercenary in the service of the Austrian emperor. Interested only in money, he kidnaps the son of a leader of the Turks in order to blackmail his father. After other adventures, the mercenary is defeated and killed by a Magyar boy. The interesting point is that the author does not depict the Turks as cruel. The foreign mercenaries are more dangerous for the Magyars. Consider this exchange:

'The emperor does not trust us.'

'Except when he is in trouble', said someone.

'And when there is a real fight. Then die, Magyar! But the foreigners are staying in the fortresses'.

It is hard to decide whether Istvan Fekete expressed a general feeling, using a situation often described in Hungarian literature, or whether these lines had a special connotation when they appeared in 1937.

After the fall of the Ottoman Empire, the Hapsburgs became the main enemies of the Hungarians who, over three centuries, were rebelling against them. The lives of our great historical personalities are linked to those of the Hapsburgs, notably in books for young readers about patriots such as Miklos Zrinyi, Ilona Zrinyi and Ferenc Rakoczi. Ilona Zrinyi defended the fortress of Munkacs (now Munkacevo in Ukraine) for two years against the Austrian forces. Her son, Ferenc, prince of Transylvania, led the army through the longest war of liberation against the Hapsburgs, between 1704 and 1711. This war is a recurrent topic in children's books. The rivalry of the Magyar soldier, Kuruc, and the Austrian Lablanc is at the centre of the action. Often the cunning Kuruc is the winner. Lablanc, a mercenary, becomes the comic figure, so that the stories have the flavour of folk tales.

The favourite book of Hungarian children is *The Captain of Tenkes* by Ferenc Orsi (1967), adapted from the film of the same title. Baron Colonel Eckbert Eberstein is sent by the emperor Leopold I to Siklos in the south west of Hungary to clear this region of rebellious Kurucs, notably a famous general, Adam Beri Balogh, who is wont to adopt various disguises so as to trick fat Eberstein and his major, Bruckenbacher. I quote the first scene in the story.

> *'I will smash them to pieces in two weeks', the colonel flared.*
>
> *'Do not think too much of yourself! This is not a normal war such as one would lead against the French army. These are Hungarian. A difficult case!'*
>
> *'In two weeks I will report the execution of the order to you, and I will attach Adam Beri Baloch to the report. Dead or alive he will be here.*
>
> *'Then in three weeks you will be a general', smiled the minister encouragingly.*

The scene continues with the colonel happily winking at the coat of arms above the door. He felt that the emperor's eagle had turned both of its heads to him, and with its four eyes would watch his deeds so that he would lead the obstinate Magyars to the faith of his Majesty. Everything turns out differently, of course: the obstinate Magyars do not want to obey the colonel and they trick Lablanc. This Kuruc period of our history had many adventurous incidents which became adventure tales. *The Two Beggar Students,* by Kalman Miksath, published in 1885, has remained in print. President Theodore Roosevelt visited Hungary to meet Miksath, whose tales he much enjoyed.

We cannot ignore Janos Hary, the 'Hungarian Baron Munchhausen'. A poem about him, *The Veteran,* was written in 1843 by Janos Garay. Hari became the main character of an opera by Zoltan Kodaly (1926). More people are familiar with the opera than with the poem. Here, the Emperor is the good, understanding 'father, like the head of a simple peasant family, with many noisy children and a warm-hearted wife. Even the two-headed eagle is tamed here. While paying a visit to the Viennese court, Orzse, Hary's sweetheart, feeds it seeds as if it were one of her chickens at home. These stories, told in local alehouses, convey the feelings of Magyars, that good relations with Austrians are simply fairy tales. In them the Magyars are always on top, a dream rather than a reality.

The war of independence, 1848-9, unified Hungary against the Hapsburgs. Written during this period, the novels of Mor (Maurus) Jokai embrace the whole of Hungarian history, the entire territory and every minority. He was very popular in his lifetime; his novels were widely translated. Queen Victoria was enthusiastic about his works. Two of his famous fictions are *The Baron's Sons* (1869) and *The New Landlord* (1983). The first became compulsory reading in school after 1945 and remains so because of its revolutionary spirit. The second was a curriculum text from 1899 until 1945 because of its conciliatory spirit and is now being revived. *The Baron's Sons* (originally *The Sons of the Stonehearted Man*) is an epic of the war of Independence. The stonehearted baron educated his three sons as loyal and faithful Hapsburgs. After his death, his wife rejects his last wishes and brings her sons home to fight in the revolutionary war. In this complicated, romantic tale we find at least three representations of German soldiers: the cruel enemy, the worthy enemy and the revolutionary brother in arms. In terms of national identity, this novel shows just how complicated it is to sort out what counts in terms of affiliation and loyalty.

The New Landlord is the most controversial but also the best of Jokai's novels in terms of aesthetic values. The hero, the new landlord, is Baron Ankerschmidt, a retired Austrian general who bought an estate in Hungary after the defeat of the Magyars and settled there with his two daughters. The baron's neighbour is an old Magyar revolutionary who, in passive resistance, never leaves his house. This man is full of prejudice about Austrians; he hates them and the whole post-war regime. His nephew, Aladar Garanvolgyi, is imprisoned in Kufstein, the most infamous Austrian prison, where many brave Magyars have died over the centuries. Gradually, the newly settled foreigners and the old inhabitants become loyal friends. Ankerschmidt and his daughter, Lisa, successfully petition for Aladar's pardon. At the time of a great flood, Aladar and his stubborn uncle save the lives of the Ankerschmidts. The marriage of Lisa and Aladar completes the reconciliation. Contemporary readers recognised the likeness between the character of Ankerschmidt and General Haynau, who, in fact, bought an estate near the river Tisza and dared to wear Hungarian national costume. So the novel unleashed a storm of protest, and yet it almost certainly helped to prepare the way for the compromise treaty between Austria and Hungary in 1867.

The New Landlord has particular relevance to current situations and feelings. Ankerschmidt built his new, fashionable house without regard to local conditions and style. He hired foreign workmen who were unfamiliar with the environment, with the result that the house collapsed in the flood. But he also learned from his mistakes, became reconciled with his neighbours and recognised the need for mutual trust between strangers. Ineffective ideas about national identity are prolonged by defining words such as German, Austrian, Ottoman, Russian, used to categorise people according to inherited prejudices. Some images change over decades, but others enter juvenile litera-ture. Books like *The New Landlord* offer alternative experiences to show that the better we know each other, the more likely it is that our stereotyped semantics will change. Hence our belief in education.

The 20th Century

After World War II, the stereotypes abolished by Jokai, Herczeg, Gardonyi and others returned, although not in the best literary forms. At the beginning of the 1950s, the period of the personality cult of Stalin, the image of a shout-ing paranoid Nazi soldier and the smiling Russian distributing bread to the starving children of Budapest was quite common. The books of the time fol-lowed the Russian-Soviet pattern. A typical example, called 'schematic literature', is the book by Laszlo Hars, *The Children Will Do It (Majd a gyerekek),* published in 1946 and revised 1955, a good example of 'social realism' in children's literature. It is modelled on the novel by Arkadij Gajdar, a Russia author, whose *Timur and his Team* was prescribed for authors of children' books at that time.

Fortunately, we have excellent books that express the feelings of Hungarians against the wars and Nazism. One of the best is the novel by Ferenc Santa, *Az otodik pescet* (*The Fifth Seal,* 1963). This book is read by highschoolers, but its philosophical aspect makes it difficult.

The best novel for adolescents, especially girls, is Magda Szabo's *Abigail.* The heroine is the daughter of a general who, foreseeing that the Germans will overrun his country, puts his daughter, for safety, in a college famous for its rigid discipline. The girl doesn't understand his motives, hates her environment and is at odds with her classmates. When the Nazis occupy Hungary, the general is arrested and sent to Germany. The Nazis try to kidnap the girl, but the pedantic headmaster refuses to give her up to anyone except her father, thus saving her life. Another teacher, a member of the resistance, helps her and other Jewish girls to escape. For those who are unfamiliar with the events of history, the story is barely credible. In fact, the Nazis forced the Hungarian governor, Miklos Horthy, to resign, kidnapped his son and transported him to Germany. Horthy's resignation on October 1, 1944 was followed by the terror and the long siege of Budapest. Christine Arnorthy's novel, *I Am Fifteen – and I don't Want to Die* was written in French. The English translation appeared in 1956. The book has not been translated into Hungarian. Anorthy is an emigrant author living in Belgium.

Reflections

The appearance of events such as these in historical fiction show that there is no single image of Germans in Hungarian literature for the young. We see the intriguer, the troublemaker, the evil enemy, the honest enemy, foe or friend at a given point in time, as the creation of a single author. However, that does not mean that there are no stereotypes.

Literature for young people tends to simplify characterisation that strongly depends on the themes and styles of any particular genre, hence the simplification that leads to stereotypical behaviour in characters and plots. In a good novel, characters are more subtly nuanced, more complex. This is the case in books by Jokai, Mikszath and Gardonnyi. This tolerant spirit was not evident in the Communist era, when the nation was divided against itself and against other nations of the world. The enforced social realism of this era encouraged the stereotyping of other nations. Hungarian readers never accepted this trend. Books that promoted it were translated from Russian, but people did not read them. Fortunately, this period is behind us.

In 1989, dramatic changes came about in both Hungary and Germany. On October 23rd, the anniversary of the 1956 revolution, free and independent Hungary was declared from the balcony of the Hungarian houses of parliament. Prior to this, the Hungarian government had lifted the Iron Curtain for three thousand East Germans who wanted to come to the West. This was an important move, which contributed to the collapse of the Berlin Wall. Hungary and Germany marched shoulder to shoulder towards freedom, and, as a consequence of the good relations developed in the last decade, Germany became the closest partner of the Antall regime. However, as we have seen in this chapter, we were next-door neighbours, but not necessarily kindred spirits.

The historical enemies – Ottomans, Austrians, Germans and Russians – belong to the past. The younger generation live in the present and for the present. Authors no longer write historical fiction; fantasies are more popular. There is no novel about the revolution in 1956. The reasons for this are complex and blurred. In 1928, Desiderius Kosztolanyi wrote:

> The books slumbering on the shelves of libraries are not complete; they are sketchy, without meaning on their own. To make meaning, you need a reader. No matter how complete they seem, in them there are only references, allusions, scribbles, which come to life in another soul. The book is always created by the writer who wrote it and the reader who reads.

Children's concepts and attitudes are included in current studies of children's literature, especially where these involve multicultural matters and feminist criticism. National identity, linked to but also distinguished from nationalism, has appeared on this scene, together with studies of children's responses in different countries to the same texts. There will be more for us to consider, soon.

Conflicting Fictions:
national identity in English children's
literature about war

Carol Fox

In England at the turn of the century, the quest for a recognisable national identity is provoking some anxiety. While Scotland and Wales take possession of new devolved parliaments, appearing to define themselves distinctively as Scots or Welsh citizens, the English, uncertain about *who they are,* are suffering an identity crisis. When politicians attempt to capture the elusive English identity they resort to nostalgia. John Major's vision of the post-mistress by the village green calls up the literature of Agatha Christie or, for children, Enid Blyton; or crude nationalism.

Jingoism aside, literature is a major medium for nation-defining. More seriously for schools and teachers, the English National Curriculum has been the site of a struggle to find a national identity for the English that is educationally and morally acceptable, with literature and history as the major filters.[1] Shakespeare and English classic texts have become compulsory reading for all pupils, while English history is to be prioritised over world or European history. Acknowledgement of the pluralist nature of English society means adding 'texts from other cultures' to the English canon at every stage, implying that although these must be included they are essentially marginal. While children's literature about war is capable of prising open the closed and self-regarding 'English' culture thus defined, it can also reinforce national myths and stereotypes. And now, in the wake of the report of the Macpherson inquiry into the murder of Stephen Lawrence, there is a concern that national identity, enshrined in the school curriculum must somehow, paradoxically celebrate and accept diversity and teach against racism[2].

I began a concentrated study of children's literature about war in 1996 when a Belgian colleague, Annemie Leysen, from the Katholieke Hogeschool in Leuven, invited me, together with other teacher educators from the UK and Portugal, to become a partner in an EU Comenius project focused on children's books about war. We had noticed a flowering of this literature in

Holland, Belgium and the UK in recent years, much of it of high quality and potential interest to young readers and their teachers. The project's aims were to collect and annotate the available books in a tri-lingual catalogue, to produce an anthology of translated extracts from the literature in each of the three countries and, finally, to support the anthology with some practical teaching materials. At that time my knowledge of the topic was not extensive. I knew and had taught the familiar modern classics – *The Silver Sword* (Serraillier, 1956), *Carrie's War* (Bawden, 1973), *The Machine Gunners* (Westall, 1975), for example, and the English poets of the First World War had been on school and examination syllabuses since I started teaching in the early 1960s. Picture story books too were catching up with the subject of war (Raymond Briggs[4], Michael Foreman[5]) and there is now material available for young children on such subjects as the Holocaust, Vietnam and Hiroshima. In the following two years I discovered at least two hundred works of literature in English on twentieth century wars alone, written in a broad range of genres on an astonishing array of conflicts taking place in settings all over the world.

The project was multicultural in two major senses – first, as a collaboration between partners located within different languages and histories, and second, the books themselves inevitably drew in themes which had to do with cultural conflict. What was often coming through these texts were ideas around *stereotypes, nostalgia, exclusion, Otherness, cultural domination, religious belief,* and, of course, *national identity.*

As a notion, national identity is not easy to define, agree upon or exemplify. The highly regarded authors of the books under discussion tend to avoid it, especially in fiction about World War Two. It can be dangerously confused with *nationalism.* For present purposes, let us define national identity as whatever cultural characteristics a society (or nation) feels its members share that distinguish it from other groups. National identity does not have to be inherently monocultural. If a social group saw its common identity as *tolerant, egalitarian,* and *pluralist,* for example, it might have *cultural diversity* as its defining feature, which would be the very opposite of Gellner's definition of extreme nationalism, where *similarity* of culture is insisted upon as the prime condition of group membership (1998, p4). Is English national identity, as it emerges through the pages of children's literature about war, excluding in the nationalist sense that Gellner defines, or is it diverse, pluralist and therefore somewhat diffuse, giving rise to the anxiety referred to earlier?

In spite of authors' best efforts to resist national stereotyping in their accounts of what are now historical events, ideas of national identity leak through their texts anyway. Accounts for children of wartime life in England in World War Two are particularly susceptible to a certain amount of nostalgia and myth-making. These slants on events are revealed when books by authors who, born elsewhere, have come to Britain from outside, and were able to regard Englishness/Britishness through the lenses of Otherness. However, books about more recent conflicts reflect a different England, one drawn more critically than the England of 'our finest hour'.

The fact that modern Britain is a multicultural society means that there are competing versions of English history and society within children's literature (Leeson, 1985). But what is interesting is that a novelist like Robert Westall, who is prepared to take a politicised and distinctly non-populist stance on the Gulf war of 1990 (see *Gulf*, 1992), also evokes an England in his World War Two fiction which is more comfortable with itself, rather inward-looking, and recognisable in terms of popular ideas of Englishness. Undoubtedly this author's ability to communicate a feeling of historical period in his books accounts in part for these two Englands. But there is also something in the way English children's authors write about the second World War that is mythical and nostalgic, possibly reflecting the way the English wish this period of their history to be thought about.

Children's literature about World War Two is mostly historical/autobiographical fiction. Those who write after the war is over look back on real events and interpret them as stories on behalf of generations who were not there. Such interpretations can range from familiarly stereotypical, sentimental and nostalgic versions (in other words the national myths that settle around great events) to critical, probing and alternative versions. For example, do the books portray England as a haven for Jewish and other European refugees, or do they explore the attitudes of the English to 'outsiders'? Is the defeat of Nazism in the War presented as an international enterprise? What did evacuation do to children? What happened to Irish nationals who refused to join the Allied forces?[6] Which stories tend to prevail?

Not all fiction for children on World War Two is nostalgic or uncritical. The books that aren't, often written from the point of view of outsiders, help us to see what is going on in the others. Books work for children at many different levels and there is nothing wrong with a good adventure story set in wartime. It is also arguable that even if children's books do embody national myths these can be subjected to a critical reading by encounters with other books. Since children's ideas of their countries' histories, of European and world history too, are an important part of their education and since literature is a very powerful medium, perhaps reading about war in schools needs to be a multi-genre enterprise in which children encounter history, autobiography, diaries, fiction and poetry. This would have the advantage of giving the readers contrasting ways of knowing, as well as foregrounding the purposes of different genres, thus gaining a greater critical purchase on texts.

A further complexity of this discussion is the readership of the books. Some were written for adults but would be accessible to young people: Briggs' *The Tin Pot Foreign General and the Old Iron Woman* (1984), for example, or Art Spiegelman's *Maus* (1986); others are written for young children but would challenge the interpretative skills of older readers (Wild's *Let the Celebrations Begin* (1991) or Gallaz' *Rose Blanche* (1985). Of these examples, all but Spiegelman's books use the familiar conventions of children's folk-tales, and folk-tales always simplify; stereotypes are their currency, the source of their enormous power. But all four books are strongly critical of war, politicians, nationalism and national rhetoric. Recounting battles as folk-tale is a part of the myth making that settles around accounts of war in all cultures. But these authors employ the forms of myth/folk-tale to speak against populist ideas of events rather than to contribute to flag-waving, sabre-rattling and the depiction of whole peoples as either victims or bullies.

One thing is certain: the greater the distance from the events narrated, the more likely authors are to make use of recognisable national symbols, to use the signifiers that have come to stand for this or that period or setting. Some outstanding books for younger readers illustrate this point. *In Flanders Fields* (Linda Granfield's picture book, created around John Macrae's famous World War One verses) pictures the poem in a stylisation which would be familiar to anybody who has seen magazines, children's books and advertisements from the early part of the twentieth century. Using these lenses to depict the horrors of the first world war has certain consequences. It gives readers a greater distance from the events, places them firmly in a not-now context and almost conveys a 'heritage' view of the Great War. I would go so far as to say that it bathes the carnage of that War in a kind of burnished glow that may help to 'protect' younger readers. By contrast, Art Spiegelman's *Maus,* not written for children but employing comic-book devices which children will certainly recognise, does the opposite. The cats and mice of his true Holocaust story are drawn in a modern idiom, communicating that the people depicted are like us now. Spiegelman's father's memories are interpreted by the author not through the illustrative styles of the 1930s and 40s but through a modern consciousness. Both Spiegelman's and Granfield's books are highly stylised representations of *memory* .

The main way we define national identities is by contrast to others. War literature for children, even when it is set in the England/Britain of World War Two is necessarily, if it is to be historically sound, full of 'others': immigrants, refugees, allied soldiers, exiles, prisoners of war. Books vary enormously in the extent to which others, however defined, are brought in. In Theresa Breslin's *A Homecoming For Kezzie* (1995), the protagonist, Kezzie, is a young woman visiting Clydeside from her home in Canada. Kezzie befriends an Italian family who for years have run a wonderful cafe near the docks. Although this book is set in Scotland (unusually for a British war story), the Italians are defined in fairly stereotypical ways – they have the love of their extended family, they cook large, appetising meals, they sing, they are emotionally warm and effusive. They are clearly 'other' and appeal to Kezzie, an outsider, because of this. But then the father and older sons are interned as Italian nationals, a disaster for the family and for the community who rely on the cafe to cheer up the bleak wartime days. The Italians' loyalty to Britain is as unquestionable as their Italian identity, and the author positions her readers to feel Kezzie's outrage at what seems pointless and destructive injustice. At this point the Italians become Britons, part of what Britain is and includes – indeed part of what it has always included. Breslin tells this story through non-British eyes (Kezzie's) and sets it outside England.

Judith Kerr's autobiographical trilogy *Out Of the Hitler Time* (1971, '75 and '78) is quite split on the relationship between the host country, this time England, and refugees. On the one hand England is a refuge from Nazi Germany for her family; on the other she does not give an anodyne or glowing account of what that meant. West London, where the family live in an assortment of hotels and houses during the war, is a melting pot of refugees from all over Europe, whose 'otherness' is in contrast to the familiar Englishness of the English that the reader will bring to the book. In Adèle Geras' *A Candle in the Dark* (1995), Clara and her brother Maxi, two German Jewish children, arrive in an English village in 1938. The author tries to show how complex their reception was: they are welcomed and well-treated, but they are also non-members and join a society which is not free of antisemitism, nor comfortable for outsiders, a theme also dealt with rather more starkly in Ishiguro's adult novel, *The Remains Of the Day* (1989). Anne Karpf's autobiography, *The War After* (1996) gives a highly critical account of what it was like for an English Jewish child of Holocaust survivors to grow up in a post-war society which seemed to demand of Jews assimilation to Englishnesss. Of the few children's books that acknowledge the presence of the British fascist movement in the East End of London in the 1930s is Jon Blake's *The Sandbag Secret* (1997), a story atypical in that it is not about the evacuation of city children to the English countryside but about how they coped with the London blitz.[7]

The East End of London has been a literary signifier for centuries. The cockney part of English national identity in literature has been well documented (Keating, 1971). Criminal, comic, chipper, poor, dirty and using strong language, the stereotypes are well-known and present in classic works (*Oliver Twist* and *Pygmalion* have both become popular musicals which modern children will have seen). The countryside, by contrast, has been seen as embodying wholesomeness, health and a settled sense of the social order. Evacuation stories of World War Two in England often perpetuate these traditions, for it was city children who were placed in country villages.

Goodnight Mister Tom[8] (Magorian, 1988), a modern classic text, is an interesting example. The sense of a strong social order in this novel, where adults know their place in the scheme of things and are respected for it, calls up George Eliot's *Silas Marner*. Silas is also an exile from an industrial city where he has been subjected to cruel injustice, and it is the village of Raveloe which, through all his moral transformation, restores and heals him. Mister Tom, the old man who, against his own will and better judgement nurtures the traumatised and intimidated young boy, Will, was played in a 1999 TV version by John Thaw, the actor who is known for his role as Inspector Morse, the Oxford detective who embodies some of the most stereotypical English characteristics – emotionally repressed, inventive, conservative, sexually inhibited, classically educated. The misguided fanaticism of Will's mother, which leads to her cruel abuse of her son, can be read in *Goodnight Mister Tom* as a metaphor for the genocide of the Jews in Europe. Will may be saved by Mister Tom, but Zach, his Jewish friend, is not so fortunate, dying not in Hitler's death camps but in the London blitz. In the same vein, Rachel Anderson's *Paper Faces* (1991) depicts an inadequate and far too young London mother, Gloria. The story of her life in London during and after the war is told with unusual realism, always through the eyes of Dot, her young daughter. Instead of presenting stereotypical London working-class characters (comic, criminal), this novel shows from inside the family what they are up against – privations of a severity that would be shocking for modern children, dealt with unpatronisingly and sympathetically.

So far I have tried to show, with the few examples that space allows, how often conflicting notions of national identity weave in and out of some very good children's stories of World War Two, sometimes slotting into established adult literary traditions. Children's literature also employs the national myths about World War Two in more expected ways. Dunkirk is the action of World War Two most often referred to, though it must be said that references to fighting are sparse in most of the fiction. A recent picture storybook, Louise Bordern's *The Little Ships* (1997) narrates the story of Dunkirk as a poem set in Michael Foreman's full-page illustrations. The tone is elegiac, both in the words and pictures, partly because it is told with the fresh simplicity of an innocent young girl, wholly without triumphalism. The book's very last page, outside the story, prints a section of Churchill's famous speech 'We will fight them ....etc'. The story and the speech each supplies a context for the other. In some ways the book represents myth making in the best sense of that practice, as stories of the past are told to children sitting at the feet of their grandparents. The only danger of such stories, in terms of national identity, would lie in their being made to encapsulate some spurious national characteristic. In *Scrapbook* (HMSO, 1989), a compilation of British forces' newspapers and magazines of World War Two, Dunkirk is reported at the time in an extremely low key. Photographs show that a regiment of Indian soldiers was part of the allied armies stranded on the beaches. Most of children's literature about World War Two excludes the presence of anyone who isn't British from the setting. USA forces, for instance, were present in large numbers all over Southern England and East Anglia but are curiously absent from almost all evacuation stories, as are allies from the Commonwealth. The danger of these absences is that they may reinforce a narrowly Anglo-Saxon view of English identity by depicting historical events as a national rather than international effort.[10]

Fiction about recent conflicts contrasts dramatically with World War Two literature, particularly in books about the Falklands and Gulf wars. The 1990 Gulf war was a TV war for the British at home. The trajectories of Scud missiles on our TV screens towards their targets in Baghdad were like the computer war games many children play. In his novel *Gulf* (1992), written very soon after the events referred to, Robert Westall gets his readers to imagine the lives of young Iraqi soldiers in the conflict. Every night, the boy who is the main character, Figgis, by a super-imaginative ability that he has becomes Latif, a terrified young Iraqi soldier. While Figgis' father and brother are glued to the TV screen with macho and certainly nationalistic enthusiasm, Figgis experiences the war at first hand, as it were, and from the point of view of the Other, the enemy. Figgis has a breakdown; Latif dies. Unlike his earlier books about World War Two, Westall's stand against the British role in the Gulf war is unequivocally critical, politically positioning British readers against their nation's involvement.

Politicians are given roles in *Gulf,* but in Raymond Briggs' *The Tin Pot Foreign General and the Old Iron Woman* (1984) they are central, with Galtieri and Thatcher grossly caricatured as monstrous fairy-tale baddies. Again TV is seen as the medium of political propaganda in this comic book, the medium through which British people 'rejoice' and participate in 'victory'. Briggs' satirical fairy-tale has the freshness and anger of a response to events at the time that they happened. In *Ethel and Ernest* (1999), which is essentially a memory of the past, Briggs shows the lives of his parents during the Second World War. The details of the pictures will be recognisable to any English person alive at the time, and there is a certain gentle and affectionate nostalgia in the way they are drawn that is part of the myth the English have made of their memories of the blitz.

Nostalgia and myth-making do not seem to be present in stories about the War written in English but set in other parts of Europe, nor in the Dutch and Flemish books identified by our Belgian partners. Lathey (1999) has pointed out how much more realistic and darker in tone these stories tend to be than their British counterparts. One way, however, that national stereotypes come into the British and Dutch books across Europe is in their depictions of Germans, usually as soldiers rather than civilians. Children's authors have been rightly concerned to distinguish between Germans as a national group and Nazis as a political group. *Friedrich* (Richter, 1971) and *My Childhood in Nazi Germany* (Emmerich, 1991), a novel and an autobiography respectively, show powerfully how ordinary German people became caught up in Nazism, but outside of such German accounts children have to distinguish between 'good' Germans and 'bad' Nazis through the good German soldier, who makes an appearance in a good deal of children's fiction. In *Morpurgo's Waiting for Anya* (1990) he is part of the occupying forces in a Pyranees village; he is friendly and helpful to the children in the story well beyond the call of duty. He also appears in Shemin's *The Little Riders* (1963), again as part of the occupying force in Holland. This time he is not only friendly, a flute player with a love of music and a family of his own at home, but he is subversive of his own role as an enemy soldier. This character also appears in Dutch and Belgian literature of the War. He can seem a cipher, a stereotype who helps children to think of German people as individuals.

However, a reading of Szpilman's *The Pianist* (1998), an autobiography of the Jewish Polish author's survival in Warsaw during the war years, brings the good German soldier into sharper focus and made me think differently about his appearance in children's literature. In Szpilman's account he is Wilm Hosenfeld, and extracts from his diary of the war years are printed after Szpilman's text. Szpilman was and is a musician, and it was Hosenfeld's love of music that drew him to Szpilman when he discovered him hiding in the ruins of Warsaw and that led Hosenfeld to save Szpilman's life. Here we are dealing with not a stereotype but a real person who gives an account of himself recorded in his own words at the time.

National identities are generalisations, and, inevitably, stereotypical characterisations of histories, people and settings. Some children's literature simplifies things, so that children can understand them. However, adults can do much to help children towards critical readings of texts about war. Among them I would suggest a multi-genre approach, wide reading of groups of books rather than one text (particularly in examination syllabuses), introducing literature in translation to bring in other perspectives, and extensive reading of adult literature. And that elusive English national identity? The whole notion seems tied up with a nation's past, its history and the stories it wishes to pass on to its children. Looking at children's literature of war, especially when it is written after the passage of forty or fifty years, helps us to see the past ideas of ourselves that we hold on to in the present, but it doesn't help us to identify who we are now. We can only observe the processes of transmission and help children to see how they happen.

This article is based on work done as part of the project War and Peace in Children's Literature, a Comenius project funded by the EU, and a collaboration involving the following participants and institutions of Higher Education:

Annemie Leysen and Annemie deWynck, Katholieke Hogeschool, Departement Lerarenopleiding, Leuven, Belgium

Raquel Gutterez and Manuela Fonseca, Ecola Superior De Educacao, Instituto Politecnico, Setubal, Portugal

Rob Batho, Faculty of Education, Chichester Institute of Higher Education, UK

Carol Fox and John Clay, Faculty of Education, University of Brighton UK

Contact: email: c.fox@brighton.ac.uk

Notes

1   DfEE English In the National Curriculum

2   The 1999 Macpherson report (Stationery Office) on the murder of Stephen Lawrence. The black 18 year old was stabbed to death by a group of white youths while waiting for a bus in South London. His killers have never been brought to justice. The report blames institutional racism in the police and in the wider society for Stephen's death and the subsequent bungled investigation of the murder. The report precipitated demands for better anti-racist education.

3   *War and Peace in Children's Books* (Eds: Batho *et al*) Leuven 1988. Copies available from Carol Fox at the University of Brighton, UK.

4   Raymond Briggs' works about war are written for adults – *When the Wind Blows* (1983) – nuclear war; *The Tin-Pot Foreign General and the Old Iron Woman* (1984) – the Falklands war of 1983; *Ethel and Ernest* (1999) – includes a section on World War Two.

5   Michael Foreman has produced three recent books about war: *War Boy* (1989), *After the War was Over* (1997), both autobiographies of World War Two, and *War Game* (1993), a story of World War One. He is the illustrator of many more, among them *The Little Ships* by Louise Bordern (1998) – Dunkirk, and *Farm Boy* by Michael Morpurgo (1998) – World War One.

6   See *The Whispering Cloth* (1995) Pegi Dietz – Vietnam; and *The Hiroshima Story* (1983) Toshi Maruki

7   See also *Street of Tall People* Alan Gibbons (1996). This children's book tells the story of the Battle of Cable Street, a confrontation between Oswald Moseley's fascist blackshirts and East End Jews, anti-fascists and communists.

8   Interestingly, the TV version was given an adult slot in the TV schedule and reviewed as a play for adults.

9   This much-quoted speech is often looked back upon as a national rallying cry.

10   Of many English stories of evacuation listed in *War and Peace In Children's Books* none includes allied USA forces stationed in Britain, though they do appear in Michael Foreman's *War Boy.*

Children's books discussed

Anderson Rachel (1991) *Paper Faces.* Oxford, Oxford University Press

Bawden, Nina (1973) *Carrie's War.* 1991 London, Heinemann Educational

Blake, Jon (1997) *The Sandbag Secret.* London, Franklin Watts

Bordern, Louise (1997) *The Little Ships.* London, Pavilion Books Ltd

Breslin, Theresa (1995) *A Homecoming For Kezzie.* London, Methuen Children's Books

Briggs, Raymond (1983) *When the Wind Blows.* Harmondsworth, Penguin

Briggs, Raymond (1984) *The Tin-Pot Foreign General and the Old Iron Woman.* London, Hamish Hamilton

Briggs, Raymond (1999) *Ethel and Ernest.* London, Cape

Emmerich Elsbeth (1991) *My Childhood In Nazi Germany.* Hove, Wayland

Feeney Josephine (1996) *Truth, Lies and Homework.* London, Penguin

Foreman Michael (1989) *War Boy.* London, Pavilion Books

Foreman Michael (1993) *War Game London.* Pavilion Books

Foreman Michael (19) *After the War was Over.* London, Pavilion Books

Frank Anne (1947) *Diary of Anne Frank.* 1990 London, Heinemann Educational

Gallaz, Christophe (1985) *Rose Blanche.* London, Cape

Geras, Adèle (1995) *A Candle In the Dark.* London, A & C Black

Gibbons, Alan (1996) *Street of Tall People.* London, Orion Children's Books

Granfield Linda (1995) *In Flanders Field.* London, Gollancz

Imperial War Museum (1989) *Scrapbook.* London, Her Majesty's Stationery Office (HMSO)

Karpf, Anne (1996) *The War After.* London, William Heinemann

Kerr, Judith (1971,75, and 78) *Out of the Hitler Time.* 1994 London, HarperCollins Children's Books

Magorian Michelle (19 81) *Goodnight Mister Tom* 1988 London, Harmondsworth Penguin

Maruki, Toshi (1983) *The Hiroshima Story.* London, A & C Black

Morpurgo, Michael (1990) *Waiting For Anya.* London, Heinemann

Morpurgo, Michael (1998) *Farm Boy.* London, Pavilion Books

Richter, Hans Peter (1961) *Friedrich.* 1978 London, Heinemann Educational

Serraillier, Ian (1956) *The Silver Sword.*1990 London, Heinemann Educational

Shea, Pegi Dietz (1995) T*he Whispering Cloth.* Pennsylvania, Boyd Mills Press Inc

Shemin, Margaretha (1963) *The Little Riders.* 1990 London, Walker Books

Spiegelman, Art (1986) *Maus: a Survivor's Tale.* New York, Pantheon Books

Szpilman, Wladyslaw (1999) *The Pianist.* London, Victor Gollancz

Westall, Robert (1975) *The Machine Gunners.* 1996 London, Heinemann Educational

Westall, Robert (1992) *Gulf.* London, Methuen Children's Books

Westall Robert (1990) *The Kingdom By the Sea.* London, Methuen Children's Books

Westall, Robert (1989) *Blitz Cat.* London, Methuen Children's Books

Westall, Robert (1984) *A Time of Fire.* London, Pan Macmillan Children's Books

Wild, Margaret (1991) *Let the Celebrations Begin.* London, The Bodley Head

The Fading of French Nationality?

Francis Marcoin

In France, children's literature has always clearly reflected national
identity; this was regulated by the Church and the State. In the second
half of the nineteenth century the question of national identity: how the
French differed from the English, for example, was a pre-eminent source of
inspiration for writers. The two nations were rivals as conquerors of the
world, especially in India. Many French writers dreamt that France might re-
claim this continent. At the end of this same century, after Germany defeated
France in 1870, patriotic feeling was at an emotional high point, and many
periodicals and other publications were called *Petit francais*. On another
level, the French saw themselves as different from the Asian and African
people they had colonised, whom they regarded as poor and inferior.

Little by little this situation has changed as the result of decolonisation, reconciliation with Germany and immigration. We now talk about political
correctness, implicitly or explicitly, and we have a new discourse of respect
for others, equality, and the idea that children are born into an international
community. *Nation* is now a negative word; *patrie* seems out-of-date, old,
comic, crazy or even sinister. In their modern life-style, young people don't
accept the idea that wars and conquests are worth sacrifices. A foreigner is
no longer an enemy or an inferior but, instead, is someone different. Difference has become a value. In an earlier work about children's literature and
the making of an expert reader, I showed how difference is emphasised in
social and communal life (Marcoin in Cotton, 1996). Even witches and ogres
are no longer the wicked.

In fact, when I began to consider this topic, I assumed that the words *France*
or *French* were missing from, or devalued in, modern children's literature. I
made a list of recent children's books where I might examine my supposition.
Here it is:

Daniel Pennac (1992) *L'Evasion de Kamo (Kamo's escape)*
Thierry Lenain (1990) *Un Père pour la vie (A Dad for Life)*
Susie Morgenstern (1989) *Les Deux moitiés de la vie (Two Halves of Friendship)*

Yvon Mauffret (1986) *Pépé la boulange (Grandad the baker)*
Nicole Ciravegna (1979) *Chichois de la rue des Mauvestis (Chichois from Mauvestis Street)*
Nicole Ciravegna (1989) *Chichois et les copains du globe (Chichois and the global gang)*
Nicole Ciravegna (1993) *Chichois et les histoires de France (Chichois and the history of France)*. (Details in bibliography.)

These writers are all extremely well known. Pennac writes for children and adults. His book *Comme un roman,* an essay on reading (translated as *Reads Like a Novel*), is a bestseller. So too is *La Fée Carabine,* not intended for younger readers, but distinguished by its treatment of 'young values'. The hero, Benjamine Malaucène, an intellectual, lives in the Belleville district of Paris, a lower class area that is a melting pot of different races and cultures. The smell of Belleville is 'a light touch of sausage and mint'. For the writer the ideal community is one where people are distinguishable by their differences, often exotic ones. Malaucène's friends are an old African (ex-native Senegalese infantry), a Serbo-Croat, who acts as an uncle to the family, a Franco-Vietnamese police inspector, and men from the Magreb: Hadouch ben Tayeb, the hero's childhood friend, and Simon from the mountainous region of Algeria. They play the three-card trick and cheat, for they are the kings of the game from Belleville to La Goutte d'or. They haven't many pals.

In contrast, in *Un Père pour la vie,* Tomate is a sad boy, withdrawn, tormented by guilt, who lives in a depressing dormitory town where the walls are grey and smell of urine. In the shopping centre, the guards are dressed like soldiers in a war film. Family violence is rife. It is a tough world, not distinctively French but conveying more generally a sense of deprivation and lack. Tomate meets a tramp, a social outcast with no fixed abode, who lives in a cabin made of sheet metal. The tramp becomes his friend. The novel has no praise for modern civilisation.

The subject matter of the Chichi series is less robust. The author, Nicole Ciravegna, was born in Nice and lives in Marseille where the stories are set. 'Chichois' is a nickname for Francois; Mauvestis, the name of the street, is an old form of the word that means 'ill-clad'. The illustrator, Colline, is also from Marseille; he does sketches for newspapers, *Le Provencal* and *Le Soir.* From the cover of *Chichois and the Global Gang* we learn that 'Chichois lives in Marseille with the rest of his family. In his class are many children from all over the world. The prettiest is Soumaia. The biggest is Bombana. The one with the funniest name is Attila Kizil...'

Because his school is a world, Chichois is confronted by children of different nationalities – all the continents are represented, except Oceania. There are three Algerian boys, one from Martinique, an Armenian, a girl from Paris, a Turk, a Spaniard, three Algerian girls, a girl from Portugal, three Corsican boys, one from Vietnam, three boys from Marseille, a Greek girl, a Chinese boy, three girls from Marseille'. All of them have splendid names. Their skin colours are all different, but their speech is interchangeable because they all have a Marseille accent. We see how the author designates them as 'a girl from Paris', 'a boy from Lyon', or 'someone from Marseille', but doesn't say they are French. The city of Marseille is the real melting pot; it is *in* France, not France itself but another France, open to the world. Soumaia comes from both Algeria and Marseille; she is more familiar with plane trees than palm trees.

The story is presented as Chichois' diary; it reviews all the problems linked to difference among the nations. Are white men really white, or are they beige? Not so white as a hand towel, surely. As for Mon-Mon, who is a nice chocolate colour, he has trouble in persuading the others that when the sun is strong, he too can be sunburnt. Ciravegna also deals with the topic of local customs: Adelene Perle from Paris calls the Spanish boy, Pablo Vasquez, 'a cruel wild beast'. In Spain, people are enthusiastic about bull-fights, and these also take place in Arles and Nimes in the south of France, not far from Marseille, so it is not an insult. I-Ko, the cleverest boy in the class, comes from China where, the teacher tells the others, the compass was invented. Racist expressions in common use show embedded prejudices: 'as strong as a Turk', 'as drunk as a Pole', hair 'as black as Chinese ink' and so on.

On Sunday, all the families walk along the Canebière, the main boulevard of Marseille. Many people there, mostly Arabs, have no car to take them to the countryside. Chichois' grandmother likes Arabs because she was liberated by a soldier from Morocco at the end of the Second World War. This soldier re-conciled her to all foreigners, except Germans. But members of a school class from Germany make it plain the young Germans are also pacifists.

This novel represents a little Utopia where everyone is interested in other people. All the children want to be friends with Mon-Mon, the only black boy in the class. But he chooses Nguyen Yan, who is Vietnamese. The Turk and the Armenian are friends, but they hide this from their parents. The book offers a model of integration that occurs in school, slowly, by means of dis-cussion and comparison among the children, rather than in lessons. In these books we have a prefiguration of the kind of language that became popular in France in 1998 when France won the World Cup, thanks to Zidane, a player from an Algerian family living in Marseille. He typifies integration '*à la français*'.

When a question is raised about roots or origins, it is usually about where the foreigner or stranger comes from. For instance, in Pennac's *L'Evasion de Kamo*, Kamo's mother has travelled far to track down her ancestors. Her grandmother was Greek; her grandfather was from Georgia, her father (a Jewish tailor) from Germany. She became a naturalised French citizen, but she doesn't feel she belongs anywhere. She falls asleep as French and wakes as Russian. To Pennac and his fellow writers the world is inconceivable without the stranger who is also our neighbour.

In *Les Deux moities de l'amitié* Susie Morgenstern arranges a particular kind of meeting between a Jewish girl and an Arab boy. They are both only children: Salah from a modest family, (seven people in a small apartment), Sarah from a wealthier one, (three people in a large house with a garden). Looking for a friend, Salah telephones at random and encounters Sarah, so they get to know each other. Their names are similar. Both are proud of their origin. Salah loves his name: Salah Abdesselem. Majestic and dignified, it suits him. Before Salah was born, his father lived in a little room. He didn't speak French and was lonely. Sarah, writing a paper about someone she admired, describes her grandfather, a hero who narrowly escaped death in Auschwitz. He has kept his Polish accent. Her grandmother, born in Constantinople, didn't know when her birthday was. She learned French at school but speaks 'Ladino', a Latin dialect, at home.

An Arab and a Jew, both feel that something separates them. People say '*sale bougnole*', (dirty wog) and '*sale juif*' (dirty Jew), and for both of them Christmas is not a feast day. Each discovers the other's identity. What exactly is it to be Jewish? Salah reads books about Auschwitz; they both read Anne Frank's diary. Sarah reads about Mohammed and discovers that the Arabs spread Greek culture and brought algebra to Europe. Salah wants to share Sarah's tastes. He asks at the public library for *La Maison des petits bonheurs,* a novel by Colette Vivier, which she likes. He devours the book, although he hadn't been much of a reader before.

> His mother, half-proud, half-troubled by her son's literary exploits, says to him: 'You're really French, you are'. Here's that word again, *French*. The children ask the question: Are you happy to be in France?' Sarah's father says it's good to live in a democratic country. Salah, who wants to use the telephone at will, says to his mother: 'That's what people do in France.'

So France reappears, not as a nationalism but as a place where people meet other people. There are Algerians, Marseillais, Jews, Bretons, tramps, but perhaps, no French. We are *in* France, a mixture of peoples.

In *Chichois et les histoires de France*, Ciravegna revises the version of history that has been at the heart of the teaching of the nation's schools, the one that gave Gallic ancestors to all French children, even if they were black. Instead she gives an account of human history, beginning with pre-history, when 'nation' as a word had no meaning and Ethiopia was in the same situation. What about the Sumerians who invented writing? Now that more is known about the history of the Gauls, the writer describes their way of life, not the wars.

So France is now presented differently, and the French have to find their roots in their other diversities, in the provinces. In *Pépé la Boulange*, the 72 year-old grandfather who has been living in Paris decides to go back home to Belle-île in Brittany, which he left when he was twelve. His grandson says: 'Life is strange; I am here because of a war, a defeat and the meeting of a girl from Flanders and a little baker from Brittany'. His grandfather avoids motorways, meets and speaks with old friends, eats genuine old-fashioned bread.

In *Un Père pour la vie*, the hero leaves his dormitory town and goes to see his grandfather who lives in the provinces, where the family has its roots. The train is a *micheline,* an old rail car invented by the Michelin company, that slowly wanders through the countryside. This grandfather lives in a house surrounded by trees. Every year, all the family come from different parts of France for a great feast. So France is also geography: provinces, landscapes climates, grandfathers who like walking. Even in *L'Evasion de Kamo*, the family of the narrator spends its holidays in Vercors, a rural, mountainous landscape near the Alps, where they lead a provincial life, old French in style, in the fresh air.

Again, we find the traditional opposition between Paris and the provinces. Despite a hint of the cosmopolitan in the charm of Melissi, Soumaia and other girls with exotic names, provincial France is shown as a refuge from violence and trauma. In all these books we find the shocks that accompany accidents and wars, and render memories problematic. Auschwitz gives the Jews an identity, racism identifies Arabs, poverty distinguishes tramps, but the chimera of a 'normal' life on the republican model of an integrated nation persists, despite literary denials.

So I cannot really write, as I expected to do at first, of a fading French nationality. No matter that discussions try to be free, modern, relaxed, the traditional values are preserved, even illustrated, in these books. Although the big towns appear to provide interesting dramatic space for writers, the writers themselves find rural life attractive and interesting. France is regarded as a country with problems, but these are much smaller than those in America. In *Ailleurs rien n'est tout blanc ou tout noir*, the story is told by a young girl, Frankie, whose parents are separated. Her father is French but was born in America. She is happy to return with him to Seattle, but she discovers that young Americans know nothing about France. They are not even sure the French have electricity. London seems more familiar to them.

This book reflects the surprise experienced by French people at foreigners who know little about their country. But Frankie discovers that 'beautiful America' has an immigration policy based on mistrust. In college, young people discuss matters relating to Indians, African Americans and Hispanics. A girl calls playboy Linwood: 'Hitler' because he wants to 'leave the Indians on the reserves, Africa to the black Africans, Mexico to the Chicanos, the United States to the Whites'. Linwood's family organises parties where racist slogans are displayed. The Blacks are also racist and violent to children of other minorities, such as the Puerto Ricans. This is the same theme as the one discussed in relation to the novels of Ciravegna but tougher when transported to America. To speak *from* America, as Frankie does, is to imply that the same situation can occur in France with the emergence of different communities. However strong the praise for 'difference', the republican ideal reappears. Therein lies the topic, the problem, of French identity.

PART THREE
Distinctive Identities

Here are three studies by writers who have strong attachments to the literary traditions of their homeland and, at the same time, are open to transcultural understandings of 'the voices of the world'. Each one demonstrates the strengths of rootedness, which new literary forms, especially in books for children, modulate and reform. Poetry for children has never been a closed system; nursery rhymes and popular songs travel on global airwaves. Modern poets, following their predecessors, appreciate a young audience. Now that they have closer access to a wider following they actively seek the frankness of children's responses to verbal play, tricks and surprises. Morag Styles has always rejected the notion that poetry is an optional extra in children's education, seeing it as fundamental to their views of themselves and others. Her commentary on selected poems extends and supports Seamus Heaney's assertion that poetry has to be 'a working model of inclusive consciousness'.

Folktales are part of local culture, everywhere. Whether or not we agree with Tolkein that they have become children's literature 'by accident', they continue to provide the young with specific, memorable examples of the universality of narratives. Carla Poesio shows how modern Italian stories continue the themes and extend the echoes of earlier tales, particularly as the result of Italo Calvino's collection, which brought together the riches of different regional traditions. The universality of this oral art form, and its susceptibility to variation and invention, underwrite the hope that children's literature can be a means of promoting a 'common' culture.

Robert Dunbar is also deeply implicated in the traditional literature of his homeland and its evolution in modern stories for young readers. He knows how the conventional stylisation of 'the Irish' ignores or conceals the colonised origins of Irish popular fiction. The legendary heroes of his country are regularly invoked to present its identity. In discussing current literature, Dunbar explores the 'tensions between history and imagination', with special reference to 'weirdness'. In this text we have a detailed exploration of the roots of a national literature, largely oral; how it represents a particular need for national identification and the forward hope of literacy for all. He warns us that the 'pace of change' in his part of Ireland 'has been so fast that it is probably unrealistic to hope for its absorption into a children's literature'. There is, of course, another Ireland, to the north, where writers for the young have followed the long, long, ideological conflicts and written books, for teenagers especially, which reflect a larger hope for the future, while reminding us that inequalities in social systems have an equally lengthy litany in folk tales.

'Voices of the World': National Identity in British Poetry for Children

Morag Styles

Not only is the notion of national identity tricky and contested, but what it means to individuals is extremely variable. Poets, like the rest of us, may feel strongly about national identity or may not be conscious of it as a defining idea in their lives, and those for whom it is significant believe in a whole range of versions. Whereas Ted Hughes writes directly about what it is like to be English, both in his choice of imagery and his deliberate use of Anglo Saxon language (as do Seamus Heaney about being Irish, Gillian Clarke about being Welsh, and Kathleen Jamie about being Scottish, though in rather different ways), poets like Charles Causley write with equal passion about one small part of England, the county of Cornwall in his case. Cultural and national identity are also important ideas in the work of many black and Asian poets, particularly those who came from Africa, the Indian sub-continent or the Caribbean, but made their homes in Britain.

What then constitutes national identity in poetry written for children as we enter the twenty-first century? It could be argued that the themes pervading current poetry for young readers are about anything and everything *except* national identity. Much contemporary poetry seeks to amuse its audience while addressing issues of social and personal concern. Superficially, the poetry is funny and light-hearted, but closer scrutiny reveals the willingness of modern poets to get their readership to think about serious issues, such as threats to the environment, endangered species, war, racism, poverty and social disadvantage. At a more personal level, many poets will tackle the consequences of divorce and other ills of childhood: difficulties at school, isolation, abuse, and the effects of racism and sexism. Children's poetry is buoyant at the moment, as sales in bookshops testify. It is to the credit of the poets that many successfully combine first-class entertainment of the young while engaging their hearts and minds in challenging topics of interest to them. A poetry of personal identity and social concern could be said to be one of the hallmarks of English poetry for children at this time.

Margaret Meek, however, remembers that in her youth 'poems were the absolute site of Englishness[1] and even the poetry of my own Scottish school-days in the 1950s contained many overtly nationalistic English poems (*The Burial of Sir John Moore, If, The Charge of the Light Brigade*), as well as the canon of Burns, Scott and Hogg. Poems against the English were especially popular, though they were fuelled by England's past cruelty against Scotland rather than dislike of fellow English people. Burns' *Scots Wha Hae* is a typical example of a rousing nationalistic poem, which is still fairly well known in schools today:

> Scots, wha hae wi' Wallace bled,
> Scots, wham Bruce has aften led,
> Welcome to your gory bed,
>   Or to victorie.
>
> Now's the day and now's the hour;
> See the front o' battle lour!
> See approach proud Edward's power –
>   Chains and slavery

In the opening poem of his first collection for children in 1979 (shared with Michael Rosen), Roger McGough gives this theme a new spin, from the English point of view this time, in *A Good Poem*:[2]

> I like a good poem
> One with lots of fighting
> in it. Blood and the
> Clanging of armour. Poems
>
> against Scotland are good,
> and poems that defeat the French with crossbows.

But times have changed and heroic verse, especially if it comes with connotations of England and imperialism, is no longer fashionable with adults or children. One reason for this is the countless manifestations of the economic and cultural globalisation that social scientist Anthony Giddens discussed in his 1999 Reith lectures.[3] On a similar note, Seamus Heaney charts his journey from 'the child in the bedroom listening simultaneously to the domestic idiom of his Irish home and the official idioms of the British broadcaster', and going on to 'the wideness of language'.[4] Paradoxically, consciousness of globalisation and, perhaps, the anonymity that goes with it, can have the opposite effect on individuals, encouraging particularistic identification with what Giddens calls 'localist', ethnic or religious groups which provide security for their followers in an uncertain world. The recent history of Kosovo and Northern Ireland are extreme examples.

Non-English national identity

If we consider national identity in Britain as a whole, we are reminded that our 'united kingdom' is composed of four distinct nations: 'England, Scotland, Ireland, Wales; All tied up with monkeys' tails', goes the old song. Indeed, Scottish, Welsh and Irish poets frequently allude to their own countries with pride and draw attention to distinctive features of their cultures in their poetry. What they also have in common is a history of conflict with their bigger, wealthier and more powerful neighbour, so it is not unexpected that whatever separates fellow Scots, Irish or Welsh, there is a common bond and purpose in unifying against England. Although this trend is more evident in poetry for adults, there is also a strand in poems for the young. Jackie Kay, for example, makes fun of the English as Sassenachs, (a Scottish word for the English to mock or despise them).[5] Here are two young lassies on their first trip to London:

> *Finally we get there: London. Euston;*
> *and the very first person on the platform*
> *gets asked – 'are you a genuine sassenach?'*
> *I want to die, but instead I say, 'Jenny!'*
> *He replies in that English way –*
> *'I beg your pardon,' and Jenny screams,*
> *Did you hear that Voice?'*
> *And we both die laughing, clutching*
> *our stomachs at Euston station.*[6]

In *Say That Again*, five Welsh poets writing for young people draw on the same themes and issues of contemporary British poetry mentioned above. Nonetheless, this book is essentially Welsh and has many reference points, cultural features and nationalistic feelings that relate specifically to Wales. Iwan Llwyd, for example, writes in Welsh as well as English. 'Sure you can ask me a personal question', the poet replies to an ignorant English interviewer, then sets about mocking stereotypes while insisting on an authentic distinctness in being Welsh:

> *No, I am not a member of a male voice choir.*
> *I have never played rugby nor worked down a pit.*
>
> ....
>
> *No, I didn't graduate in Dylan Thomas's work.*
> *Yes, many of us do drink too much*
> *Some of us can't get enough drink.*
> *This isn't a minority face,*
> *This is my face.*[7]

Scottish, Irish and Welsh nationalism apart, I have scrutinised contemporary children's verse to see if there are any remnants of nationalistic feeling left and tried to probe what, if anything, has replaced it. My tentative conclusion is that, although current English poets are rarely nationalistic, many celebrate regional and cultural identity, which I shall discuss more fully. Before I do, it is useful to mention the poetry of the past in this respect. The great names in children's poetry before the twentieth century – William Blake, Anne and Jane Taylor, Edward Lear, Lewis Carroll, Christina Rossetti, Hilaire Belloc – wrote poetry which was recognisably English, whether through channels as various and implicit as pastoral landscape, the excoriation of eighteenth century London, or the development of nonsense, cautionary verse or nursery rhymes.

Class and National Identity

Robert Louis Stevenson was Scottish, but his outstanding collection, *A Child's Garden of Verses* (1885), distinctive in so many other ways, did not stand out in terms of national identity.[8] His bourgeois garden could easily be an English one. However, there is some sense in the poems of the otherness of children from foreign countries. Stevenson is not xenophobic, quite the opposite, but in *Foreign Children* he shows the prejudices of his time, even if his tongue is in his cheek:

> You have curious things to eat
> I am fed on proper meat;
> You must dwell beyond the foam,
> I am safe and live at home.
>
> Little Indian, Sioux or Crow,
> Little frosty Eskimo,
> Little Turk or Japanee
> O! don't you wish that you were me?[9]

Stevenson's garden was a privileged one, not open to the poor nor relevant to the experience of working class people. Similarly, A.A. Milne's verse is probably the last to present a clear sense of national identity in that the poems are set in an upper-class English nursery. The charm of the verse, say some critics, blinds the readers to the way Milne makes them feel superior to the lower orders, as in *Buckingham Palace*:

> They're changing guard at Buckingham Palace –
> Christopher Robin went down with Alice.
> Alice is marrying one of the guard
> 'A soldier's life is terrible hard'
> > *Says Alice.*
> They're changing guard at Buckingham Palace –
> Christopher Robin went down with Alice.
> We saw a guard in a sentry box
> 'One of the sergeants looks after their socks,'
> > *Says Alice*
> They're changing guard at Buckingham Palace –
> Christopher Robin went down with Alice.
> We looked for the King, but he never came.
> Well, God take care of him, all the same,'
> > *Says Alice.*[10]

Alice uses non-standard grammar and holds a simple view of life. She fantasises about the elite while remaining only a naive onlooker. Embedded in the verse is a conventional, respectful view of royalty, typical of Milne's day. Alternatively, Alice could be seen as an appealing, fresh, ironical voice, distancing herself from the symbols of nationalism and the trappings of royalty that go with it.

Contrast this with Jamaican/British Benjamin Zephaniah writing in the 1990s, who mocks the Queen in poem after poem:

> Dis ting is serious   God save
> Do it for all of us   Our
> Save our asparagus,   Green[11]

Milne, whose poetry has many merits and is still enjoyed by young children seventy-five years after it was written, was at one time editor of *Punch*, a magazine which, in its time, was almost a byword for Englishness, so it is not surprising that his children's verse took on some of those qualities, which were further accentuated by E.H. Shepard's delightful but conservative illustrations. Today, a significant number of English poets writing for children come from less privileged backgrounds; others are keen to stress an all-encompassing invitation to readers from every class, race and creed and to set their work in an urban context, the experience of the vast majority of young readers.

Regional Identity

If most English poets do not now emphasise in their work a sense of England as a nation, many show affection for a particular region. Charles Causley is the outstanding example. His poetry is peppered with references to his native Cornwall and its traditional folklore. His first collection for children, *Figgie Hobbin,* is actually the name of a Cornish pudding. This is the first of many mentions of places, characters and old tales:

> My young man's a Cornishman   His eye is bright as Dolcoath tin,
> He lives in Cambourne town,   His body as china clay;
> I met him going up the hill   His hair is dark as Werrington Wood
> As I was coming down.   Upon St Thomas's Day.[12]

Causley brings his beloved Cornwall alive for the reader, who both learns about it and grows to appreciate its special musical qualities. He has continued to draw on this rich vein in many superb volumes of poetry for children, including *Jack the Treacle Eater* (a Somerset man, this time) and *The Young Man of Cury* (who was the poet's Head teacher). It is a depressing speculation as to whether Causley's depiction of Cornwall, with its particular, local evocations of a vanishing past, can become part of the awareness of modern children.

Better known as a poet for adults, Ted Hughes, like Causley, devoted about half of his time to writing for children. Both poets have been heaped with honours; Hughes was Poet Laureate. *Rain Charm for the Dutchy and other Laureate Poems* (1992) although not for children, shows him at his most English. To some extent, all of the poems are about national identity, but the final line of a poem for the Queen Mother's ninetieth birthday also exemplifies what some commentators have called an 'imagined' community of belonging.

> When Britain wins, I feel that I have won.
> Whatever Britain does, I feel I have done.
> I know my life comes somehow from the sun.
>
> I hardly understand what I can mean
> When I say Britain's Queens and Kings are mine.
> How am I all these millions, yet alone?[13]

Hughes was the great English nature poet of the second half of the twentieth century and it is in his poetry of birds, insects, animals and seasons that we find a subtler trace of national identity, especially in poems accessible to young readers in the first two of the four volumes of his *Collected Animal Poems*[14] (1995) and in the 1985 edition of *Season Songs*.[15] Most of the time Hughes develops a sense of England through his detailed attention to its land and wild life. Now and again he makes a specific reference to England. There is a Devon bull in *Pets*;[16] Bess the badger[17] came from a pet shop in Leicester; and a hare is likened to a Druid soul at 'midnight on the A30';[18] in *April Birthday*,[19] he mentions the 'gently breasted Counties of England'; and the fox 'with a Robin Hood mask' who is one of the tragic heroes of *What is the Truth?* is sacrificed for the traditional English sport of hunting:

> Who
> Wears the smartest evening dress in England?
> Checks his watch by the stars
> And hurries, white-scarfed
> To the opera
> In the flea-ridden hen-house?[20]

One finds a completely different view of England in the work of Michael Rosen, one of the most popular writers, broadcasters and performers of poetry for children to-day. He is mainly seen as a humourist, but Rosen has always given attention to bewildering and difficult issues in the personal lives of children. Many of his poems are autobiographical.[21] He is not interested in a conventional view of national identity, openly displaying socialist and internationalist leanings in his work for older readers. But he often writes about his own cultural identity, in particular about being Jewish. In a recent collection, *You Wait Till I'm older Than You!* we get a tragic-comic Jewish wedding, a hilarious account of his dad cooking greasy but delicious 'matzo bray', specifically against the advice of his mother; and we meet Leosia:

> When the Nazis came in the west
> his parents put him on a train
> going east
> and he never saw them again.
> They died in a Nazi death camp.[22]

In a post-colonial setting

Ceremonial poetry apart, overt nationalism has become not just unfashionable but unfeasible because of the inescapable consciousness of the legacy of British colonialism. It is no accident that, in so far as themes linked to nationalism are addressed in modern poetry for British children, the key poets are from a generation poised between cultures which are themselves in transition. The most successful and easily identified group are those who came originally from different parts of the Caribbean and have chosen to settle in Britain. Their voices, poised as they are between changing cultures, can uniquely address the contemporary experience of living in a multicultural society with all its tensions and undercurrents, sometimes with an understandably adversarial slant, mostly with generosity and humour.

Some, like James Berry, were part of the Jamaican contingent that came to Britain in the first wave of immigration fifty years ago. They expected their 'mother' country to welcome them with open arms; they had grown up steeped in British literature and ideas. Now they encountered racism and hostility. In the 1970s, many Caribbean/British poets showed their anger and frustration in poems like *Inglan is a Bitch* by Linton Quesi Johnson and *Dis Policeman Keeps on Kickin Me to Death* by Benjamin Zephaniah, for adults, of course. Although racism is still a serious issue, Britain in 2000 is a much more integrated multi-ethnic society than it once was. Johnson and Zephaniah are now successful, mainstream writers and performers. Indeed, Zephaniah was spoken of as a possible contender for the office of Poet Laureate after Hughes' untimely death in 1998.

John Agard was the first Caribbean/British poet to produce a collection for children, *I Didn't Do Nuttin* (1984), followed a few years later by Grace Nichols' *Come on into my Tropical Garden*,[23] James Berry's *When I Dance*, and *Duppy Jamboree* by Valerie Bloom.[24] One constant feature of this poetry was the celebration of things back home, so that the poets' sense of national identity remained that of their origins. Bloom and Nichols introduce animals, flowers, food, chants, games and stories. Mothers are remembered (*Ain't have* nothing dat *me mother can't do*) and Grandmothers honoured (*Granny Granny please comb my hair*). Some of the poems use simple Creole, but their English is shaped by rhythms and idiom of the poets' places of origin, especially effective when read aloud. Edward Kamau Brathwaite, the historian and poet, coined the term 'Caribbean Nation Language', the English spoken by the slaves and labourers who were taken from Africa.[25] 'Nation language' is now used by Caribbean/British poets to hold up a mirror to white suppositions and prejudices. One of the strengths of children's poetry in Britain today is that it is willing to address the fractures, tensions and contradictions of post-colonial culture. Here is John Agard in *Checking Out Me History*

> Dem tell me wha dem want to tell me
> But now I checking out me own history
> I carving out me identity.[26]

In his introduction to *When I Dance*, James Berry says: 'When one's previously excluded cultural experience becomes naturally and properly included in mainstream learning... steps have been taken, away from pure ethnocentricity, in the direction of the human family.'[27]

Seamus Heaney discusses this tension in language when he tries to unravel poetry's obligation to challenge injustice, how it is 'pressed to give voice to much that has hitherto been denied expression in ethnic, social, sexual, and political life'. He also suggests that it is possible to have

> a poetry which consciously seeks to promote cultural and political change and yet can still manage to operate with the fullest artistic integrity. Poetry, let us say, whether it belongs to an old political dispensation or aspires to express a new one, has to be a working model of inclusive consciousness.'[28]

If his words become reality we can hope for a new emerging inclusive national identity in literature for children, reaching out to Europe and the rest of the world, enjoying difference instead of being afraid of it, realising that the cultural life of Britain and its language is enriched by ethnic, cultural and linguistic diversity. Let's sing in time with the voices of the world, like the central character of Berry's poem,

Black Kid in a New Place
I'm here, I see
I make a part of a little planet
here, with some of everybody new.

rooms echo with my voice, I see
I was not a migrant bird. I am
a transplanted sapling, here, blossoming.

Notes

1. Margaret Meek Spencer in a letter to Morag Styles, August 1999.
2. Roger McGough and Michael Rosen, *You Tell Me*, Puffin, Harmondsworth, 1979: 11.
3. Anthony Giddens, The Consequences of Modernity, Polity Press, Cambridge, 1991: 52.
4. Seanus Heaney, (1998) *Opened Ground*, London, Falmer.
5. Sassenachs is a Scottish word which can be used with humour or contempt to describe English people.
6. Jackie Kay, *Two's Company*, Blackie, London, 1992: 47.
7. Iwan Llwyd 'Sure you can ask me a personal question' in *Say That Again*, edited by Mairwen Jones and John Spink, Pont Poetry, Ceredigian, Wales, 1997: 65.
8. Robert Louis Stevenson, *A Child's Garden of Verses*, Longman and Green, London, 1885.
9. Robert Louis Stevenson, *A Child's Garden of Verses*, Puffin, Harmondsworth, 1976: 49.
10. A.A. Milne, *When We Were Very Young*, Methuen, London, 1924: 2.
11. Benjamin Zephaniah, *Funky Chickens*, Viking Kestrel, London, 1994.
12. Charles Causley, *Figgie Hobbin*, Macmillan, London, 1970/1990.
13. Ted Hughes, *Rain-Charm for the Duchy and other Laureate Poems*, Faber, London, 1992: 30.
14. Ted Hughes, *Collected Animal Poems*, Volumes 1-4, Faber, London, 1995.
15. Ted Hughes, *Season Songs*, Faber, London, 1976/1985.
16. *ibid.*, 1985: 73.
17. Ted Hughes, What is the Truth? Faber, London, 1984/1995; *Collected Animal Poems*, Volume 2: 5.
18. *ibid.*, 1995: 90.
19. Ted Hughes, *op cit.*, 1985: 25.
20. *ibid.*, 40.
21. Michael Rosen, 'Monologues and Spiels: the 'I' of my poems' in *Tales, Tellers and Texts*, eds. G. Cliff Hodges, M.J. Drummond and M. Styles, Cassell, London, 1999: 192/3.
22. Michael Rosen, *You Wait Till I'm Older Than You!* Viking Kestrel, London, 1996: 79.
23. Grace Nichols, *Come on into my Tropical Garden*, A&C Black, London, 1988.
24. Valerie Bloom, *Duppy Jamboree*, Cambridge University Press, Cambridge, 1992.
25. Edward Kamau Brathwaite, 'English in the Caribbean: Notes on Nation Language and Poetry' taken from a talk given by the author at Harvard University in 1979, quoted in *Using English: from conversation to canon*, eds. Routledge, London, 1996: 266.
26. John Agard, *Say It Again, Granny!* Bodley Head, London, 1986.
27. James Berry, *When I Dance*, Hamish Hamilton, London, 1988: 117.
28. Seamus Heaney, *The Redress of Poetry*, Faber, London, 1995: 2/7.

Flavours of Italian Tales, Yesterday and Today

Carla Poesio

The hero of Italian folktales is Italo Calvino. When a collection of two hundred examples of the genre, selected, retold and annotated by this famous novelist, was published in 1956 as *Fiabe Italiane*, its readers discovered that they now had an anthology to match any other collection of folk tales that claimed to represent a national culture. The English translation by George Martin appeared as *Italian Folktales* in the US in 1980, and in a British Penguin edition in 1982. The critics acclaimed the book as a rich cultural resource and praised the skill and subtle clarity of the narration.

By bringing together stories from different regions, dialects and story-telling traditions, Calvino shows how tales that are at the root of all popular culture become, in the written form, a literate-literacy consciousness, which then becomes 'national' when a nation claims it. Italian folktales, says Calvino, 'were recorded in literacy works long before those of any other country'. But the folktale 'never had the romantic vogue among Italian writers and poets that it enjoyed in the rest of Europe, from Tieck to Pushkin. Instead, it was taken over by writers of children's books, the master of them all being Carlo Collodi, who, some years before writing *Pinocchio,* had translated from French a number of seventeenth-century fairy tales.'

Calvino differentiates folktales for children as 'separate genre, neglected by more ambitious storytellers and carried on in a humbler and more familiar tradition with ... characteristics of coarseness and cruelty which would be considered wholly unsuitable in children's books today', perhaps in order to produce a 'readable master collection of Italian folktales which would be popular in every sense of the word,' popular, that is, with adults. But this does not exclude the possibility that other influences could be at work to link modern stories for children with tales from earlier times. Calvino's versions 'are labelled 'Italian' in so far as they are narrated by the people of Italy, tales that have come into our narrative folklore via the oral tradition; but we also classify them as Venetian, Tuscan, or Sicilian, or belonging to other Italian regions' (xxi). Yet, behind the scholarship and skill of this definitive collection lie the stories children heard, stories which had 'their roots both in fantasy and popular sentiment', as elsewhere in the world. Now, those who write stories for Italian children inherit both streams of storytelling, oral and written.

Where Calvino shimes brightly is in his awareness of the individuality of storytellers and of the ways by which the stories are identified with their region of origin. He acknowledges the part played by creativity, 'the inner poetry of the stories', whereby 'the timeless folktale is linked with the world of its listeners and with history' (xxii). In his account of Agatuzza Messia, who was the model narrator for the Sicilian collector, Giuseppe Pitre (1841-1916), Calvino appreciates her colourful narratives, active female characters and her ability to 'conjure up magic' derived from 'a picture of the condition of the common people'. In contrast, he is also drawn to the variety of early cultural influences in Tuscan folktales collected by Gherardo Nerucci (1880), whose storytellers narrate most of the important tales from Montale, a village near Pistoia in 'a harsh, mangled, violent Tuscan' which Nerucci reproduced in his version.

Despite the undoubted attraction the voices of the tellers have for Calvino, he separates himself from those of his predecessors who sought the origins of folktales in a so-called 'scientific' historicism based on compared recurrences of motifs and types. Instead, he offers his readers a broad glimpse of the past, then creates the conditions for modern reading of the texts which best 'defined the spirit of the age' of the early storytellers, taking care to distinguish the originals by naming their regions (xxv). A continuing point of reference for the whole range of storytelling is, naturally, Boccaccio's *Il Decamerone*.

One of the most important of Calvino's sources is *Lo cunto de li cunti o vero lo tratteniemento de peccirille* (*The Tale of Tales*), written between 1634 and 1636 by Gianbattista Basile, a Neapolitan who brought together, in his splendidly baroque Neapolitan dialect, certain features derived from oriental folktales and the stories told by his fellow citizens. Like Boccaccio and Chaucer, Basile has a 'frame' tale, a cover story in its own right, which links the others. Following the folktale scholar Stith Thompson, Calvino says that the last tale in *Il Pentamerone* may be the only one of 'probable Italian origin'. But in these oriental tales we find an alchemy of linguistic expressions, customs, behaviour, costumes, milieux, all of which transform the characteristics of their source into something completely new. A German version of this work appeared in 1846 with a foreword by Jacob Grimm, and a part of it was translated in England by Edward Taylor in 1848, by which time the nineteenth century revival of folk and fairy stories was well under way.

If we look at what has happened more recently to fairy and folktales since the renewed growth of interest in oral storytelling, we see that the motifs discerned by earlier scholars are now a matter for discussion in terms of the 'diachronic stages of transformation', as demonstrated by Dieter Richter in *La luce azzurra* (Mondadori, 1995). He points out the recurrent transmission of motifs in forms of 'multimediality': poems, novels, theatrical performances, of which opera is a good example (English readers may think of the 'reclaimed' folk tales of Angela Carter, the studies of Marina Warner, and the transformations of popular folk and fairy tales by Disney). Among Richter's examples is a story by Basile, *Il corvo* (The Raven). Its tragic theme of faithful friendship recurs in Lorenzo Lippi's heroic-comic poem, *Il Malmantile riacquistato* (Florence 1676) and again in 1761, this time as a popular drama by Carlo Gozzi, *L'amore delle tre melarance* (*The Love of three Oranges*), which also provided Prokofiev with the text for the libretto of his opera of that name (1919). In 1777-8, the editor and scholar Johan Gottlieb Schlimmel published *Kinderspiele und Gesprache* (*Children's Games and Sayings*), which included a theatrical composition, *Der Raben* (The Raven), another elaboration of Basile's tale. There are two versions in Calvino's collection.

Calvino's scholarly comment and his subtle narrations make it impossible to miss the vital distinction of Italian folktales: the nature of magic, the characteristic which joins these old tales with their modern counterparts for children. Magic, in Italian tales, is the way by which the hero or herione can change his or her destiny. At the same time, it brings about what is both necessary and longed for: food, money, greater strength, but also more subtly, rebellion, especially of the underprivileged. Calvino points out that the hero often wins freedom for others as well as for himself. In Tuscan tales, it is often the heroine who shows this kind of courage, as in the tale of Fanta-Ghiro the Beautiful, who became 'queen of two kingdoms'. The conventional nature of story-telling, ages old, also lets the storyteller invent new versions of the confrontations of rich and poor, young and old, worthy and unworthy. Magic extends the range of choices to be made by both characters and readers at each turn of the tale.

The continuing role of the storyteller is the link between the traditional folktale and its modern counterpart, whether the readers are adults or children. Within the conventional forms, the narrator makes a personal choice of story ingredients, while keeping his or her personal voice and rhythm in the narration. Modern Italian writers, notably those we consider here, select tales from the folktale legacy more or less deliberately to support their theme or motif, at the same time keeping some individual synchrony and harmony with their sources.

Gianni Rodari (1920-1980) was responsible for a deep renewal of Italian children's literature after the Mussolini regime and the Second World War. He is an excellent example of an author interested in folk and fairy tales, as both narrator and essayist. As a sincere adherent of the Communist Party, Rodari was bound to privilege the social aspect of folktales, including the courage necessary to take initiatives. But he did not spoil the freshness of his plots nor the surreal attraction of his magic, the elements that linked him with older storytellers and with political propoganda. His stories emphasise the common possibility of forging for oneself a better destiny. Liberation from a state of slavery or from unjust subjugation are constant themes in traditional storytelling, as is the possibility of imaginative escape fromn the routine daily drudgery of modern life. These are also typical of some of Rodari's stories, especially in the tale *L'autobuss no. 75* in his collection of *Favolae al telefono* (*Fables on the Phone*). I choose this as an example.

An overcrowded bus sets off at the beginning if a hectic working day in Rome. Without warning, it changes its route. The passengers are scandalised and furious. After much protest the bus stops in the open countryside. Still complaining, the passengers leave the bus. Gradually they respond to the beauty and calm of their surroundings and to the chance to relax, to chatter, to play. But all too soon the bus takes them back to hustle-bustle of the city streets. Was that small taste of freedom only a dream? In *Favole al telefono*, the stories are grouped in a 'frame' tale about a father who, working as a travelling salesman, calls his daughter every evening to tell her a bedtime story. The stories are short; there is not much money for phone calls. In this frame we see elements of Boccaccio, Chaucer, Basile and *The Thousand and One Nights,* of evening storytelling, family gatherings of rich and poor.

The echoes of traditional tales and attachment to their magic makes the surreal in Rodari's stories seen a legitimate poetic licence. Rodari has a subtle sense of humour, something almost entirely absent from children's books of the fascist period. (Humour is always dangerous for hegomonies.) Critics greeted it as a precious element of renewal in Italian children's literature, recognising its link with its earlier counterpart in folktales, especially the Tuscan and Neapolitan ones.

Humour in a tale of social concern is also characteristic of the work of **Bianca Pitzorno,** one of the finest Italian contemporary writers. Her *L'incredibile storia di Lavinia (Lavinia's incredible story)* seems at first to be a retelling of Andersen's *The Little Match Girl*. It begins with a child match-seller, alone, cold and hungry in a big city where people are shopping frantically on Christmas Eve. A fairy getting out of a taxi gives Lavinia a magic gift, a small iron ring which, when turned, transforms everything she longs for and cannot have into dung. Thus, the archetypal function of a magic ring, the satisfaction of desire, is changed into a kind of punishment of adults who do not understand the legitimacy of children's longings. On one occasion at midnight, when an unsympathetic shopkeeper refuses to give Lavinia a pair of shoes for her bare feet, Lavinia turns the ring and, at the same time, looks intently at the shoes. What the shopkeeper then sees on the shelf is a little heap of smoking excrement. This scatological element, not at all rare in folktales, is part of a succession of comic transformations to punish those who frustrate children's hopes and expectations. But Lavinia, the traditional sorcerer's apprentice, is carried away by the power of the ring. No longer poor or forlorn, she uses it to indulge herself. The greed and consumerism of the big city intoxicate her. The happy ending is provided by her restorative friendship with a boy who works in the luxury hotel where they are both unhappy.

Authors differ in their borrowings from traditional tales. **Guido Quarzo** is a case in point. His adaptation of older motifs and situations provokes questions about retellings; why are they so fashionable in comtemporary children's literature? Is he, like other authors, showing the continuous relevance of ancient plots or 'postmodernising' archetypes for fun, or are they playing games with readers? Are they suggesting that confrontation, comparison and evaluation between past and present bring about deeper, more interpretive readings? Quarzo makes an original blend of these activities. He revivifies archetypal metamorphoses with brilliant humour, reminding his readers that the traditional Italian folktale was strongly influenced by Ovid and Apuleio di Madaura *(Amore e Psyche)* in the recurrent interaction of high literature and oral storytelling. Sometimes, as in this tale, his readers are given a clue to his starting point.

Each time he falls in love, the hero of the *Seconda storia del principe faccia di maiale (The second story of Prince Pigface)* is transformed into a monstrous creature with a snout. But he does not await the kiss of a young girl to restore him. Instead, a magician proposes to the Prince a series of travels which bring him experience, confidence, self-respect and a change in his appearance. His resemblance to a pig almost disappears. Flavoured with pure humour, Quarzo's writing never fails to emphasize, with a light touch and some changes in conventional motifs, the common sense which is an essential part of the traditional folk or fairy tale.

One of Italy's most talented writers, **Roberto Piumini,** exemplifies Calvino's maxim about Italian folk tales: 'A quiver of love runs through them'. *I portatore di baci (The Bearer of Kisses)* is a delicate love story. A young lady asks her page to carry a kiss to her husband who has been waging war far away from home. The kiss has a stronger effect on the page than on the proposed recipient. This tale and others are set in a metahistorical epoch between the middle ages and the renaissance and coloured by sentiments derived from the tradition of chivalry and the French troubadours. There are echoes of the *Chansons de Geste*, which have their special place in the Italian tradition. The influence of Italy's greatest romantic epic, Ariosto's *L'Orlando Furioso* (1532), is also clear. Familiar to storytellers all over Europe and another example of the links between high literature and popular culture, the inexhaustible fantasy, the power of love and humour in this great poem, all resonate in Puimini's fiction.

All the works of this many-styled writer, who offers his readers a range of settings, periods, motifs, are distinguished by the rhythm of the narratives. Music, sounds and noises are central to the semantic strength of *L'ascoltatore di muri* (*The Man who Listened to Walls*) (1982). Leaning his ear to the wall of an old gothic church, a Dutchman hears a sweet mediaeval chant amongst confused rustlings and buzzing noises that indicate the passing of the centuries. Extravagant as this opening may seem, the story that follows, of how the listener devises a means to distinguish the counterpoint of a medieval chant from the cacophonous buzzing of the intervening centuries, is a metaphor for the continuity and renewal of traditional storytelling.

During his years of work to seek out and present every type of folktale, the existence of which is documented in Italian dialects, and the representation of all regions of Italy in the final collection, Calvino says he was guided by the Tuscan proverb: 'The tale is not beautiful if nothing is added to it'. In other words, its value consists in what is woven and rewoven into it. This chapter is part of that continuous reweaving of the texture of stories and of national and international cultures and identities.

Work cited

Basile, Giambattista (1632-4) English translation by Sir Richard Burton (1893) *Il Pentamerone (The Little Ones' Entertainment)*

Boccaccio, Giovanni (1350-55) *Il Decamerone*

Calvino, Italo (1956) *Fiabe Italiane*. Einaudi

Donghi, Beatrice Solinas (1993) *La fiaba come racconto*. Momdadori

Nerucci, Gerardo (1880) *Sessanta novelle popolari montalesi*. Le Monnier

Pitre, Giuseppe (1871-1913) *Fiabe, novelle e racconti popolari siciliani*. Vols 4, 5, 6, off Biblioteca delle tradizione popolari siciliane

Pitzorno, Biance (1985) *L'incredibile storia de Lavinia*. Edizioni EL

Piumini, Roberto (1982) *Storie dell'orizzonte*. Nuove Edizione Romane

Richter, Dieter (1995) *La Luze Azzura: saggi sulla fiaba*. Mondadori

Rodari, Gianni (1962) *Favole al telefono*. Einaudi

Quarzo, Guido (1990) *Seconda storia del Principe Faccia di Maiale*. Edizioni EL

Ireland and its Children's Literature

Robert Dunbar

'Mother Theresa says Ireland's a queer mixture of the old and new,' said Valerie. 'And she says it's natural in a country that's had a history of such ups and downs. She asked me to tell the class what sort of funny contrasts I'd noticed – coming from England, you see.'

'And what did little Miss Clever answer?' asked Geoff with brotherly interest.

'Well, I said for one thing it was a bit weird to see a lot of dashing modern cars on awful mountain roads driving past a stream of donkeys and carts. And I said I'd never get used to barefoot boys going into some of those very modern new cinemas.'

'But that's part of the fun of Ireland,' Geoff argued. 'You never know what you're going to see next.'

The children's book in which this conversation occurs is Maisie Herring's *The Young Traveller in Ireland*, first published, in Britain, in 1951. It is one in a long series of 'Young Traveller' titles of the period, in which the genres of travel book and adventure story merge, the primary intent being to provide child readers with some idea of a selected country's history, geography and contemporary social conditions. These are observed and reported on by visitors to the country, in this case young people from the English midlands. Two of them (Geoff and Valerie, brother and sister) extend their role as visitors to become temporary residents when, in the absence of their parents in South Africa, they go to stay with an Irish aunt and attend an Irish school. By the time we leave them preparing for their first Irish Christmas they have had more than enough opportunity to appreciate their aunt's view, as expressed in the book's closing lines, that 'almost anything can happen in Ireland'; here, clearly, as Geoff realises in our opening quotation, is a place where 'you never know what you're going to see next.' By a fascinating coincidence, a later children's book in the adventure travel mode, Hazel Greenham's *Ann and Peter in Ireland* (in *The Kennedys Abroad* series), first published, in Britain, in 1966, sells itself in its blurb as follows:

'Irresistibly caught in the magic of Irish laughter and tears, Ann and Peter take each exhilarating day in their stride. A film unit – a storm at sea – not forgetting the tale of Grace O'Malley the female pirate – anything can happen in Ireland.'

The perception of Ireland as a totally unpredictable country may seem at first to be little more than a romanticised excuse for the creation of children's fiction where no concession at all need be made to any notion of reality; the Ireland of the imagination can become a very free and easy world. Certainly, in its portrayal over the centuries by children's writers – Irish or otherwise – the emphasis has often been on its potential for the magic of the unexpected and on its status as a place apart. Wildness and eccentricity flourish, generally manifested in exaggerated characterisation, histrionic behaviour, easy sentimentality and idiosyncratic speech patterns. ('Gran' day to yer, yer honer,' gasped the farmer, running up. 'Oi saw ye a-coomin' in, an oi says to meself, says I, 'sure an' wot is it ye're afther?': this is from Moyra Charlton's 1930 story *Tally Ho: The Story of an Irish Hunter*, admittedly published when the author was in her teens.) Inevitably, the result, especially with the less gifted writer, is a descent into stereotyping, in which condescension towards the native can make itself only too obvious.

Read now with hindsight, many of these earlier young people's books dealing with Irish themes can be seen as harmless and (unintentionally) humourous period pieces. The young Irish women who feature in a number of the school fictions of the prolific Cork-born L.T. Meade – *Wild Kitty* (1897) and *The Rebel of the School* (1902) are but two examples – are invariably mischievous, unconventional and high-spirited. They may indeed be 'wild Irish girls' but it is part of their 'education' that they eventually come round to accommodating themselves to the more structured ways of a society more inhibited, apparently, than their own.

In effect, what we are confronting in the earliest examples of what may be considered Irish children's literature – books written and published before, say, 1922, when the twenty-six counties of the Irish Republic attained their independence – is proof of its bearing many of the hallmarks of the colonised society in which it originated or with which it dealt. In some cases these hallmarks are more immediately visible, in others more subtly reflected. Frances Browne's *Granny's Wonderful Chair*, first published in 1856, is usually mentioned in a footnote in histories of (English) children's literature to accounts of the late Victorian popularity of literary fairy tales and inevitably in the same paragraph which mentions the contemporary translations of Hans Christian Andersen – fairly enough, perhaps, given that in her own final paragraph Browne hails Andersen as 'one whose tales of the fairies are so good that they must have been heard from themselves.' But what is hardly ever remembered is that Frances Browne was born in 1816 in a small village in Donegal, where she spent the first thirty-six years of her life before moving to London. 'Once upon a time,' begins the story called 'The Story of Merrymind', 'there lived in the north country a certain poor man and his wife, who had two cornfields, three cows, five sheep and thirteen children,' a setting of some local veracity, one suspects. The paired characterisation which Browne favours so much – the brothers Scrub and Spare, the brothers Clutch and Kind, the brothers Sour and Civil – affords a study in the dualities typical of colonised society, with all of them competing for power and expression. Similarly, Browne's elemental and stylised settings, such as the cottage, the forest and the big house, while found in many folk- and fairy-tales, have a particular resonance when seen in an Irish context When the two daughters of the Lords of the White and Grey Castle, in the story of that name, are dis-possessed and made to tend swine, they find themselves eventually in a forest where the residing bountiful Lady tells them, 'Choose whether you will go home and keep hogs or live in the forest free with me.' 'We will stay with you,' said the children, 'for we like not keeping swine. Besides, our fathers went through this forest and we may meet them some day coming home.'

'We may meet them some day coming home.' That sentence reminds us of the pattern of separation, journey and (possible) return which we find in many of our ancient (and modern) stories: they are, of course, universal features, but have a striking appropriateness in a country where dissension, emigration and exile have featured so largely in our history. It should come as no surprise that Irish children's writers, as we shall see later, are drawn in such numbers to that history as starting points for their own journeys. But the history here is not merely the history of the textbook, rich as that has been, and continues to be, as an inspiration for the huge corpus of Irish children's historical fiction. For in Ireland there is a constant shifting ground where myth and history mingle. (What is history, asked Napoleon, but a myth agreed upon?) While that ground has always been with us, it comes into particular prominence, certainly in the context of Irish children's literature, in the period between, approximately, the 1880s and the 1920s. These are the years which were to bring Ireland's initial development from colonial to post-colonial status and which, in literary terms, saw the flourishing of what would become known as the Irish Literary Revival, when the country's most ancient stories were reclaimed, retold and related to notions of national loyalty and pride.

Many of these retellings, in the spirit of the age, were heavily sanitised versions of the originals, and not just in those intended for the young, writing for whom became a self-appointed minor task for many Revivalists, providing a kind of Irish equivalent of that branch of Victorian English chil-dren's fiction which focused on the young men (mainly) who would one day rule an Empire. It was Standish James O'Grady who, in almost single-handedly inventing heroic Ireland, first brought many of these ancient tales to a popular and, eventually, a young audience. (Yeats was to acknowledge his significance when he wrote in his *Autobiographies*: 'In his unfinished History of Ireland, O'Grady made the old Irish heroes, Finn and Oisín and Cuchulain alive again...O'Grady was the first, and we had read him in our teens' – a phrase which must be one of the earliest Irish references to teenage reading). These stories, O'Grady wrote in his *Early Bardic Literature*, 'represent the imagination of the country: they are that kind of history which a nation desires to possess' – a statement which neatly encapsulates the tensions between history and imagination which continue to characterise Irish society.

The overtly political intent of much of the Irish children's literature of the Revival period has come under recent scrutiny from commentators such as Declan Kiberd and Maire West, who have examined the role played in that literature by mythology and legend in the evolving construction of Irish national identity. But important and influential as this children's literature may have been in its time, its almost quasi-mystical emphasis on heroism and history makes much of it now seem very dated. What gives it lasting interest is its notion of what being Irish entails and, equally significant, its concern with story itself.

For a wide range of contemporary Irish children's writers these stories, now stripped of their political metaphors, remain a potent source of reference, if not necessarily reverence. (See, for examples of the irreverent, the strip cartoon versions of Larry O'Loughlin or the grotesquely humourous variants of Eddie Lenihan.) Retellings of the stories, lavishly illustrated in coffee-table book manner, appear regularly from Irish publishers. Motivated sometimes by an educational heritage agenda and sometimes by more obviously commercial promptings, such volumes tend to have strong tourist appeal. But the more literary, creative impulse stems from an attraction to what H.P. Lovecraft memorably diagnosed as 'the current of weirdness' in Irish literature. Here, in this weirdness, are the sources of nearly all our Irish children's fantasy, to be found in such earlier writers as Padraic Colum, continuing with Patricia Lynch and surviving into contemporary times in writers such as Cormac MacRaois, Michael Scott and Kate Thompson. These stories, like the oral ones which Edine Cadogan listens to at the ceilidhe in the Widow Rafferty's house in Lynch's 1941 novel, *Fiddler's Quest*, are typically 'of strange happenings and enchantments', populated by a wide diversity of real and supernatural characters. Here are fictional worlds where reality and fantasy are very clearly linked and where the picture of Ireland that emerges is of a terrain where the possibilities of magical and marvellous experiences lie around every corner. It is precisely the sort of place where the young travellers of 1951 believed almost anything could happen.

When we move from considerations of Ireland as a place where 'almost anything can happen' to considerations of it as a place where much indeed has occurred, it is tempting to return once again to the comment made by Valerie, one of our young travellers. Quoting her teacher, she saw the country as having had 'a history of ups and downs', a phrase which, while clearly qualifying as an understatement, nevertheless touches on one of the reasons why Irish history should continue to exert such a fascination as a theme for Irish children's writing. The country's centuries of historical development can easily be seen as a series of confrontations and conflicts, the stuff of which vivid historical fiction, dealing with clashing ideologies and divided loyalties, is made. In her book, *Object Lessons,* the Irish poet and critic Eavan Boland comments:

> If a poet does not tell the truth about time his or her work will not survive it. Past or present, there is a human dimension to time, human voices within it and human griefs ordained by it. Our present will become the past of other men and women. We depend on them to remember it with the complexity with which it is suffused. As others once depended on us.

The past few years have brought from Irish children's writers such as Marita Conlon-McKenna, Tom McCaughren, Michael Mullen, Elizabeth O'Hara, Mark O'Sullivan, Siobhán Parkinson and Gerard Whelan a succession of novels which set out to capture, in Boland's phrase, our history's 'human dimension' and 'the complexity with which it (the past) is suffused'. The result is a body of work which, to adopt Stephen Dedalus's well known sentence in Joyce's *Ulysses,* genuinely makes an attempt towards awaking from the nightmare that is Irish history. We encounter in the best of these books new ways of seeing the past, free from the sort of facile and sentimental clichés to which a passing professor had given voice in Greenham's *Ann and Peter in Ireland*. Asked by Ann why he thinks so many Irish songs are sad, he pronounces, 'It's the Celtic melancholy, a beautiful sadness of the soul, emphasised by the centuries of hardship and heartache, of enforced departures, and many weeping goodbyes.' These are the signposts to whimsy of a kind particularly out of tune with a modern Ireland. The point is not that we have not experienced 'hardship and heartache' and all the rest – or that they have not contributed to our being as a nation what we are: it is that we no longer have to wallow in them. As Celia Keenan has pointed out, this new Irish historical fiction for the young can be seen as reflecting 'a kind of new confidence' in Irish society.

It is not, though, the case that the mists of whimsy surrounding the island of Ireland have, in its contemporary children's literature, totally evaporated. In polarised terms, we continue to witness a confusion as to what is 'Irish' and what, derogatorily, is 'Oirish'. As early as 1946, Kenneth Reddin in an article in *Irish Library Bulletin* had delivered a spirited criticism of such writing, swingeingly dismissing its fondness for 'pigs in the kitchen and little red hens and tinkers splitting skulls down bohereens, and ass carts and clumps of turf and heaps of muck, cabins, sleans, Seáns, illiteracy, bad whiskey and general devilment. All the things we have blamed England for in her attitude to Paddy the Irishman; all the things which America loves to think make the 'rale' Irish scene...' And it is perfectly true that the paraphernalia listed by Reddin clutter and disfigure much of Irish children's literature up to (and sometimes beyond) the 1960s and 1970s. C.S.Lewis, on holiday in Donegal in 1956, wrote to an American friend Mary Willis Shelbourne, 'I doubt if you'll find any leprechauns in Eire now. The radio has driven them away'. But his suspicions of their demise turned out to be slightly premature: what we might call the leprechaun spirit was to linger on, particularly in the 'adventure story' genre of Irish children's fiction.

The first notable attempt to present a different viewpoint of an Irish setting can be seen in many of the novels of Eilís Dillon. Of her short story 'Bad Blood' in an Irish children's literature anthology, *The Lucky Bag*, published 1984, she writes, 'It shows boys on the edge of being grown up and learning to handle the good and bad aspects of being a man.' Exactly so, because what emerges strikingly in Dillon's work is a sense of, in many applications of the word, transition. The 'world' of many of the stories is recognisably the Ireland of the 1940s and 1950s, but it is a terrain (as in, say, a novel such as *The Island of Ghosts*) in which the winds of change are gently audible. Compared with later writers, there is not, perhaps, a full incorporation of the disturbance which the transitional state usually involves, but there is, at least, a tentative reaching out to embrace change. Each of the West of Ireland islands which provide most of her settings becomes a microcosm of the larger one around whose shores she places her adventures. By the time in the late 1980s when Tony Hickey's 'Joe' trilogy appears, the breakthrough from rural to urban, from idealised to realistic, has been finally made. These are hard-edged narratives, dealing (for the first time in Irish children's fiction) with shadowy, marginalised existences. They prepare the way for the first wave of young adult fiction, Irish style, which the 1990s were to bring and in which the first fictional intimations of the 'new' Ireland were to be clearly perceptible.

For those of us who live in Ireland the signs of this 'newness' are all around. There is increasing economic prosperity. Unemployment is falling. Emigration has been replaced by immigration. Conservative attitudes towards a wide range of social matters are – not without a struggle – yielding to a greater tolerance. As keen supporters of the European ideal, we are eager to see beyond our earlier parochialism. But the 'funny contrasts' noticed by young Valerie's teacher in 1951 remain. The much-vaunted Celtic tiger does not roar equally loudly for all. The United Nations 1999 Human Development Report ranks Ireland sixteenth out of seventeen Western countries, with 15.3 per cent of the population living in 'human poverty', one contribution to these statistics being the frightening revelation that 25 per cent of Irish adults cannot function at the most basic levels of literacy. Few weeks pass without some further disclosure of sexual abuse in the immediate past of our educational system or of financial skulduggery in the immediate past of our political life. As the growing number of asylum seekers, refugees and migrants move us towards a multicultural society, the early signs of racism and xenophobia are detectable. And, a few miles up the road from our capital city, there is the continuing and apparently insoluble problem of 'the north' and its 'troubles'.

There are, in truth, many Irelands in our new millennium and it is a fair expectation that as our native writing for the young develops in quantity, quality and confidence it should come to reflect and respect these pluralities. The pace of change outlined in the preceding paragraph has been so fast that it is, however, probably unrealistic to hope for its immediate absorption into our children's literature. (Indeed, the spate of 'Ulster troubles' children's fiction may prove that sometimes longer periods of reflection are preferable to a hasty desire to transmute fact to fiction.) Traditional notions of childhood and adolescence as periods to be protected from, as distinct from being prepared for, adulthood remain as inhibiting forces for some of our writers and publishers.

But for those able and willing to be more adventurous the rewards are already within sight. When Dahy, the hero of Tony Keily's 1994 *The Shark Joke*, witnesses some scenes of alcoholic misbehaviour in the city streets he reflects, 'The few tourists still around look worried about this business, because it shagged their idea of Ireland being a place full of banshees and virgins and warm pints of stout', a reflection which shows that the boy's experience of his native place owes little to earlier conventional images. Similarly, in the opening pages of Margrit Cruickshank's 1992 novel, *Circling the Triangle*, when young Stephen Russell, in the course of embellishing a friend's living room with some carefully considered graffiti, takes down 'a picture of a thatched cottage' there is a symbolic farewell being accorded to a certain vision of Ireland. The ten short stories by Ré Ó Laighléis in his 1996 collection, *Ecstasy*, afford particularly vivid evidence of a newly emerging

Irish landscape. In, 'Heredity' he portrays the claustrophobic intensity of a family cracking under severe pressure, triggered initially by the father's alcoholism and, subsequently, by his verbal and physical abuses of the mother. Caught between is Paul, three weeks away from his end-of-school examinations, gradually steeling himself into some kind of protest against his father's brutality: when the showdown comes it is for both father and son a moment of remarkable discovery.

To these examples could be added an impressive range of writers – June Considine, Maeve Friel, Peter Gunning, Bernadette Leach, Jane Mitchell, Mark O'Sullivan, Siobhán Parkinson, Marilyn Taylor, among others – who experiment in their fictions with new themes and are beginning, refreshingly, to consider new modes of telling. Not all of these books necessarily represent, in literary terms, the highest attainments, frequently because in focusing so strongly on contemporary matters the story becomes sacrificed to the issues or, in some cases, because the excitement of being free from earlier thematic and linguistic taboos results in a desire to shock for shock's sake. These, one hopes, will be short-lived aberrations and may be the price that has to be paid as a new generation of writers, following in the footsteps of Joyce's Stephen in *A Portrait of the Artist as a Young Man*, sets out to encounter the reality of experience and to forge the uncreated consciousness of this new, challenging and contradictory race. As young Geoff might well express it, you never know what you might see next.

Irish children's books by authors mentioned in text: a selected listing

Conlon-McKenna, Marita. *Wild flower Girl*. O'Brien, Dublin, 1991.

Considine, June. *The Glass Triangle*. Poolbeg, Dublin, 1994.

Dillon, Eilís. *The Singing Cave* (1959). Poolbeg, Dublin, 1991.

Friel, Maeve. *Charlie's Story*. Poolbeg, Dublin, 1993.

Gunning, Peter. *Kick the Can*. Blackwater, Dublin, 1997.

Leach, Bernadette. *4 Ever Friends*. Attic, Cork, 1998.

Lynch, Patricia, *The Bookshop on the Quay* (1956). Poolbeg, Dublin, 1995.

MacRaois, Cormac, *Lightning over Giltspur*. Wolfhound, Dublin, 1991.

McCaughren, Tom. *Ride a Pale Horse*. Anvil, Dublin, 1998.

Mitchell, Jane. *Making Waves*, Poolbeg, Dublin, 1998.

Mullen, Michael. *To Hell or Connaught*. Poolbeg, Dublin, 1994.

O'Hara, Elizabeth. *Penny-Farthing, Sally*. Poolbeg, Dublin, 1996.

O'Sullivan, Mark. *Silent Stones*. Wolfhound, Dublin, 1999.

Parkinson, Siobhán. *Sisters.. .No Way!* O'Brien, Dublin, 1996.

Scott, Michael. *Firelord*. Wolfhound, Dublin, 1994.

Taylor, Marilyn. *Call Yourself a Friend?* O'Brien, Dublin, 1996.

Thompson, Kate. *Wild Blood*. Bodley Head, London, 1999.

References

Boland, Eavan. *Object Lessons* (1995). Vintage, London, 1996.

Browne, Frances. *Granny's Wonderful Chair.* (1856). Dent, London, 1960.

Chariton, Moyra. *Tally Ho: The Story of an Irish Hunter*. G.P. Putnam's Sons, London, 1930.

Colum, Padraic. *The King of Ireland's Son* (l916). Floris Books, Edinburgh, 1986.

Conlon-McKenna, Marita. *Fields of Home*. O'Brien, Dublin, 1996.

Conlon-McKenna, Marita. *Under the Hawthorn Tree*. O'Brien, Dublin, 1990.

Cruickshank, Margrit. *Circling the Triangle*. Poolbeg, Dublin, 1991.

Dillon, Eilís. *The Island of Ghosts*. Faber, London, 1990.

Dillon, Eilís. *The Island of Horses* (1956). Puffin, Harmondsworth, 1976.

Dillon, Eilís. *The Lost Island* (1952). O'Brien, Dublin, 1986

Dillon, Eilís *et al* (ed.). *The Lucky Bag*. O'Brien, Dublin, 1984.

Greenham, Hazel. *Ann and Peter in Ireland*. Frederick Muller, London, 1966.

Gunning, Peter. *Reaching the Heights*. Blackwater, Dublin, 1995.

Herring, Maisie. *The Young Traveller in Ireland*. Phoenix House, London, 1951.

Hickey, Tony. *Joe in the Middle*. Poolbeg, Dublin, 1988.

Where is Joe? Poolbeg, Dublin, 1989.

Joe on Holiday. Poolbeg, Dublin, 1991.

Keenan, Celia. 'Irish Historical Fiction' in *The Big Guide to Irish Children's Books,* ed. by Valerie Coghian and Celia Keenan. Irish Children's Book Trust, Dublin, 1996.

Keily, Tony. *The Shark Joke*. Martello, Dublin, 1994.

Kiberd, Declan. *Inventing Ireland*. Cape, London, 1995.

Leach, Bernadette. *Summer Without Mum*. Attic, Dublin, 1993.

Lenihan, Eddie. *Fionn Mac Cumhail and the Baking Hags.* Mercier, Cork, 1993.

Gruesome Irish Tales for Children. Mercier, Cork, 1997.

Humourous Irish Tales for Children. Mercier, Cork, 1998.

Lynch, Patricia, *Brogeen and the Green Shoes*. (1953). Poolbeg, Dublin, 1989.

Lynch, Patricia. *Fiddler's Quest*. (1943) Poolbeg, Dublin, 1994.

Lynch, Patricia, *The Grey Goose of Kilnevin* (1939). Poolbeg, Dublin, 1994.

Lynch, Patricia. *The Turf-Cutter's Donkey* (1934). Poolbeg, Dublin, 1988.

MacRaois, Cormac, *The Battle Below Giltspur*. Wolfhound, Dublin, 1988.

MacRaois, Cormac, *Dance of the Midnight Fire*. Wolfhound, Dublin, 1988.

McCaughren, Tom. *In Search of the Liberty Tree*. Anvil, Dublin, 1994.

Meade, L.T. *Wild Kitty*. W & R Chambers, London, 1897.

Mitchell, Jane. *When Stars Stop Spinning*, Poolbeg, Dublin, 1993.

Mullen, Michael. *The Flight of the Earls*. Poolbeg, Dublin, 1991.

Mullen, Michael. *The Long March*. Poolbeg, Dublin, 1990.

O'Grady, Standish James. *Early Bardic Literature* (1879). Lemma Publishing, New York, 1970.

O'Hara, Elizabeth. *Blaeberry Sunday*. Poolbeg, Dublin, 1994.

O'Hara, Elizabeth. *The Hiring Fair*, Poolbeg, Dublin, 1993.

Ó Laighléis, Ré. *Ecstasy and Other Stories*. Poolbeg, Dublin, 1996.

O'Loughlin, Larry. *Fionn and the Scots Giant*. Blackwater, Dublin, 1997.

O'Loughlin, Larry. *The Gobán Saor*. Blackwater. Dublin, 1997.

O'Loughlin, Larry. *The Salmon of Knowledge*. Blackwater, Dublin, 1999.

O'Sullivan, Mark. *Melody for Nora*. Wolfhound, Dublin, 1994.

O'Sullivan, Mark. *More Than A Match*. Wolfhound, Dublin, 1996.

O'Sullivan, Mark. *White Lies*. Wolfhound, Dublin, 1997.

Parkinson, Siobhán. *Amelia*. O'Brien, Dublin, 1993.

Parkinson, Siobhán. *No Peace for Amelia*. O'Brien, Dublin, 1994.

Reddin, Kenneth. 'Children's Books in Ireland' in *Irish Library Bulletin* 7(1946)

Scott, Michael. *Earthlord*. Wolfhound, Dublin, 1992.

Scott, Michael. *Windlord*. Wolfhound, Dublin, 1991.

Taylor, Marilyn. *Could I Love a Stranger?* O'Brien, Dublin, 1995.

Taylor, Marilyn. *Could This Be Love? I Wondered.* O'Brien, Dublin, 1994.

West, Máire. (1994) 'Kings; Heroes and Warriors: Aspects of Children's Literature in Ireland in the Era of Emergent Nationalism' *Bulletin of the John Rylands Univ. Library of Manchester* 76, 3

Yeats, William Butler. *Autobiographies*. Macmillan, London, 1955.

The Englishness of English Children's Books

Margaret Meek

Forty-eight years ago when I began to write about children's books, I found myself in a dilemma when I discussed them with others. On the one hand were my learned colleagues, critics and theorists as well as experienced teachers of English in schools, whose professional interest in the reading done by young people did not extend, except in passing, to the books read out of school. Because of my enthusiasm for E. Nesbit, a notable socialist in her day, and invitations to come with me to publishers' parties, they told me about their adolescent reading. But they had little experience of the historical novelists (Geoffrey Trease, Henry Treece, Hester Burton, Rosemary Sutcliff and others) who, I said, were changing children's literature fundamentally. On the other hand, the well-read writers of children's books: their editors, dedicated children's librarians and others who knew the social history of what children had been given, or found, to read, opened new doors for me. These professionals were looking for ways to establish the importance of children's books as contemporary material productions and to widen their readership beyond the traditionally bookish middle class. Gradually the groups moved closer together. Advances in printing technology, the growth of paperback publishing and the quality of children's television adaptations made children's books more popular. Increasing emphasis on the long-term effects of early book reading, and the role of parents in supporting this, also changed both the production and distribution of texts for young people.

In terms of international exchange, however, the trade has been less than reciprocal. Whereas books in English have been widely translated, a matching awareness by UK readers of texts from non-English speaking countries has been slow, if not reluctant to emerge. For many British people who would claim to be interested in children's literature, a French book might be the stories of Babar or Asterix, Pinocchio for Italians, Grimm's tales or *Emil and the Detectives* to represent Germany, Pippi Longstocking for Sweden. I hope this ignorance is not insensitivity, but ignorance it certainly is. The success of books in English out of the UK seems to have made British readers more insular, more nationalistic, although Maria Nicolajeva (1996) suggests that that this may be a more general characteristic. Not all teenage books that originate in the US are popular in Europe, and Canadian authors want to be clearly distinguished from their neighbours. The best-known international prize for a children's book, the Hans Andersen award, has not raised the general consciousness of all readers about their insularity. So it is with some trepidation that I approach the topic of the Englishness of English children's books and some of the cultural problems they are bound to present for readers who meet them in translation. Some books written in English seem to be very Englishly English. I am aware of this because I am a Scot, living in London, displaced from the language and culture of my childhood. I am conscious that English children's books are enriched and sustained by artists and writers from all over the world, whose displacement is much greater than mine. They have had to create their identity out of a different history and culture even if they are Caribbean, for example, although English is their mother tongue, as it is mine. I notice too that the work of writers from Australia, India, Africa and North America who write in English has a certain critical edge, recognisable and significant. I mention this characteristic and believe it is important. From time to time I appropriate it for my work as a teacher, but I have to lay it aside as this chapter deals with other issues.

The general awareness of the Englishness of English children's books found in the writing of critics outside the UK is based on certain key texts, widely recognised. These serve as paradigmatic instances or defining cases for what the critics want to say about English books for children more generally. The usual examples are *Alice in Wonderland* (1965), *The Wind in the Willows* (1908), *Peter Pan* (1911), *Winnie the Pooh* (1926), *The Lord of the Rings* (1968), and *The Stories of Narnia* (1950-1956). The common phenomenon in these books perceived by outsiders is not that they are all written by men, but that they share a common fictive characteristic, called 'fantasy', to describe its Englishness. (Interestingly, J.M. Barrie and Kenneth Grahame were Scots living in England.) In fact, this set of conventions, where the 'laws of nature are suspended or amended' in order to consider the nature of possibilities rather than actualities, is common to narrative fiction in most cultures. The Englishness lies not in the choice of a particular genre, but in the details that compose it; again, something quite ordinary in all literatures. Yet somehow the fantasy label sticks to these books, especially when the critics are of a psychoanalytic bent, concerned to distil from the texts a particular view of childhood. For example, Isabelle Jan says of *Alice*:

the wonderland of this literature has a distinctive characteristic of its own that is deliberately non-realistic. Here, instead of sublimating reality in translating it into symbols, it is completely distorted. an altogether different world emerges from which all familiar landmarks have been removed, a world of pure fantasy.

Jan's praise for *Alice* is that it catches the anxiety 'typically that of a child'. This may be the reason, or one of the reasons, why many children are puzzled or distressed by the characters. and the lack of sequence in the plot. But if one begins with Carroll's own assertion that he 'just made it up while he went along', quite different evidence emerges about the perplexity experienced by a number of young readers. For one thing, no single episode is related to any other. The 'fun' is in the language play, the mocking of adults, the parody of well-known children's rhymes and poems. And there is definite threat, real and unmistakable, in the events themselves and in what the characters actually say, things that are not easy to translate because they are culturally parodic as well as linguistically so.

The first non-English book I read about children's literature was that of Paul Hazard: *Les Livres, Les Enfant et Les Hommes* (1932). I read it in 1949, after the war that completely changed the scene Hazard described when he said that 'England could be reconstructed entirely from its children's books'. At the time when Hazard was writing, the gulf between actual social life in England and its appearance in children's books was immense. In a sense, the books Hazard read kept him from knowing this. But I believe Hazard was more serious when he said that boys' adventure stories, chiefly written at the end of the last century and which he like so much, 'formed and sustained the national soul'. No one in England could write these words now, although some politicians would like to.

Here, then, are some different issues that arise in the study of the Englishness of English children's books. My examples come from a single *oeuvre*: the work of Janet and Allan Ahlberg, who began their professional careers as teachers, and discovered, in a remarkable partnership that lasted for 20 years, that they could create the kinds of imaginary worlds that children in England take pleasure in inhabiting. The books are worth closer study than we can give them in a short time so this descriptive analysis will inevitably be over-generalised. One fact stands out. The current Englishness of English children's books depends largely on the authors' and artists' realisation that books for very young children, especially those composed mostly of pictures, are successful if they address an audience of both adults *and* children, to-gether. During the early part of childhood when children are discovering what books are and what reading can be like, they are the implied audience. But the books themselves are produced, sold, bought, read and judged by adults. All the successful makers of books for young children recognise this duality as an essential part of what they do. The Englishness lies in the fact that, where this duality implies difference, most writers and artists are on the side of the children.

Children's books in England have a long, well-documented history. But here, as everywhere else, the nature and evolution of books for children has always depended on the economics of production and distribution. The English precis for this is the motto of the eighteenth century bookseller, John Newbery, who is credited with the earliest production in England of books as objects of delight and amusement rather than for instruction: 'Trade and Plum Cake for ever, Hurrah'. In 1975, after the first post-war blooming of children's books, when the Newbery tradition had been reawakened, Janet and Allan Ahlberg, whose books I have chosen for their 'Englishness', began their work together. By this time children's books had found a market in the widespread children's libraries. Also, changes in printing techniques, especially colour separation, gave artists new scope. The picture books of the Sixties, with some distinctive exceptions, were more painterly than graphic. In the midst of novelty and colour experimentation in picture books by artists like Brian Wildsmith and Charles Keeping, the Ahlbergs concentrated on a more intricate interplay of words and pictures, reviving as they did so the distinctive line of Victorian artists, and at the same time creating a different style of representation. Instead of a wider splash, the Ahlbergs offer smaller, infinitely revealing vistas of English social life and 'innerly' ideologies, recognisable not only by those who share the cultural assumption or understandings of the artists but also by others who had hitherto expected pictures in children's book simply to underline the events in the story. You have to look and read carefully, as children do, so that the words expand the images and the images 'thicken' the meanings of the words. No explanation conveys this accurately; only the books do. Adults reading with children often find their attention drawn to the fine quality of the detail. Nothing is in the pictures by accident.

Fully to appreciate the nature of Ahlberg books as material productions, it is also necessary to understand the part the authors play in their final appearance. From the early days of independent publishing, the convention was for the author to send the publisher a text, and for the publisher to find an artist to illustrate it. The text and the pictures then came together at the printers. On the whole, originators of children's books were, until recently, fairly ignorant of book production and left the details to their editors. In contrast, the Ahlbergs exploited all the technical innovations available to them: advanced paper engineering and precision binding as well as colour separation. They worked to a shared aim, with no compromise, in order to produce a physical object in which every single detail is important. The significance of this is the closing of a gap between the reader and the authors. The artisan printer, and the editor who represents the publisher, are executives whose task is to make possible the collaboration of the writer and the artist and the reader. When people speak of the Golden Age of children's books in England in the Sixties and Seventies, this is the state of the fastidious and careful publishing they have in mind. (That it also happens elsewhere is concealed from us by our ignorance of others' practices.)

The topics of the Ahlberg books are linked by various strands, threads, *filières* to 'a social situation in process of change'. Traditionally, children's books in England were part of a middle-class enclave which separated them from the popular culture of magazines, albums or 'lotteries'. The Alhbergs picked up this earlier popular history after they had examined the picture book scene in some detail. They saw, for example, how their baby daughter, aged one, turned the pages and examined the illustrations of a catalogue that came from a well-known store for children's clothes, so they made *The Baby's Catalogue*. The idea is simple; the semiotics are highly sophisticated. The hasty reader sees a series of representations of things that characterise the daily lives of young children and are easily recognised by them. Even very young readers identify what they see in the book with things that do not exactly match them in everyday surroundings (a fact that intrigues psychologists). The verbal text is apparently unambiguous: a category list of things, incidents and common events, just as in the adult model. But in the pictures. the careful adult reader discovers five families, and without hesitation can make assumptions from the details of hair, clothes, food, toys, occupations. postures and possessions about their different life styles. All the families have things in common, but only the nappies are identical. Those who buy this book, thousands of them, to read with their children before they go to school, recognise the sameness and difference as part of the whole. What I wonder, would Hazard have to say about this England? Would he see how these new authors, for all their devotion to the fine traditional 'line', actually *subvert* the actualities of childhood by simply demonstrating sameness and difference?

Let me show you another example of this gap closing in book production – this time in a social context which in England has been, and is now more than ever before, a political battleground. In the UK, the nursery school, *la maternelle*, has not been a full national educational provision. Pre-school education is common in two quite different social groups: the comfortable middle-income families, and those with special 'social need'. The UK National Literacy Trust – a non-governmental body – has a long list of projects that now encourage links between home and school so that parents may collaborate with teachers about the adjustments children have to make between these two socialisations. In 1987 a teacher in the local school where the Ahlbergs' daughter was to be a pupil, asked Janet and Allan to help her to make a little booklet to explain the routine of the school day to the parents of children who were about to go there. (The usual procedure now is that the parents learn what the school is like by visiting it with the child.) The pamphlet became a book that parents and children could read together. It shows what this school is like, so that the parents and children can talk about a place that is not exactly where their child will be going but has general similarities. The young readers and their parents can discuss the experience of going to school in advance.

The book is called *Starting School*. The print simulates children's early writing and the pictures create a recognisable representation of local primary schools. The individual differences of the children are quietly and equally celebrated. The events occur one day at a time and then week by week, as the rhythm of familiarity increases. The order and the occasional turmoil of school life are acknowledged without insistence. When the book appeared, some commentators were disappointed that there was too little emphasis on equal opportunities, a theme much discussed at the time and a distinctive one that permeates all serious studies of children's books in England, with repercussions throughout the United Kingdom.

No study of English children's books can ignore the issue of *class*. It is the most pervasive aspect of social life in England, historically and contemporarily. It includes a subtle network of social, linguistic and literary codes that entwine children's books and the development of their readers as literates. There are many families who would not recognise their children as belonging to the group that go to the Ahlberg school. As for the outsiders, the poaching readers, we need a long apprenticeship in both big and small literatures to understand the ramifications of class significations and differences. Insiders, those who understand class oppositions almost instinctively, especially as these are replicated and supported in our school system, look to authors of books for children to be even-handed. We can see from the detailed drawings, again, in their presentation of children from different cultures, that the Ahlbergs are aware of this, but the suggestion from outside is that this tokenism is not enough to make any real difference in social attitudes more generally.

If, however we look at Allan Ahlberg's texts in other books, especially in poems and stories, we see his awareness of the inequalities of English childhood quite clearly. The hero of *Burglar Bill* (1977), perhaps his most popular early tale, helps himself to what he sees and desires ('I'll have that!'), only to find that a stolen box with holes in it contains a baby. Bill's Cockney speech does not meet the criteria set by the National Curriculum for English:

> 'You married, Bill?' says Burglar Betty.

> 'No' says Burglar Bill. 'The right woman never come along.'

Young readers know that the dialectal forms in the text are subversive rule breaking of the code. They also know when to shout 'I'll have that', the refrain uttered by Burglar Bill himself as he goes about his business. (He is reformed in the end by the appearance of Burglar Betty, but many parents are uneasy about the stealing appearing in a book for children). Likewise, in *Please Mrs Butler* (1983) a book of poems which are instantly appealing to the young, the inequalities and unfairnesses of school are sketched lightly, but unforgettably. I doubt if there is a single reading teacher in England who does not understand the Englishness of that poem, 'I-am-in-the-slow/readers-group' and its relevance to the failure of many children in the early years to come to terms with the literacy demands of schooling. It would take more pages to explain than there are in this book as a whole. Allan Ahlberg's representations of children's social awarenesses are a particular kind of sub-version, the kind of sub-versions that children themselves make of their world.

Here we pick up another strand. The history of children's literature in England begins, like all other literatures, in the oral tradition of singing and storytelling. English nursery rhymes are formally acknowledged as 'heritage' and are upheld not only by the children themselves but also by various forms of scholarship. The most recent of these is the 'discovery' by two Oxford psychologists that nursery rhymes teach children learning to read 'phonological awareness' and thus help them to learn to spell. Amongst children, nursery rhymes are a common orality, but those you learn may depend on where you learn them, and on whether or not you understand the unorthodox parodic versions.

In *Each Peach Pear Plum*, this old nursery rhyme is transformed into a story game, 'I Spy', one all children know. In the book the reader has to find the characters in the pictures. Thus, Mother Hubbard is represented by the back view of her dress; Cinderella's duster is the clue to her whereabouts. The Three Bears out hunting (in English sporting tweed) cause an accident to Baby Bunting whose rescue involves Robin Hood, Bo-Peep, Jack and Jill and the Wicked Witch, all of whom are hidden in the careful drawings of the countryside before they emerge to contribute to the happy ending. The subtlety is that the landscape, portrayed as picture at the beginning of the book, comes into closer focus and is framed on each page, bit by bit, as the story goes on. The authors expect that the readers will already know the characters from the nursery rhymes, or will simply find them out. So there are two kinds of 'spying': the first is the recognition of the nursery rhyme characters in the pictures; the second is the readers' realisation that those who made the book also know Tom Thumb. In the same way readers of Jane Austen know, when they meet another reader, they just have to say Elizabeth Bennet, and the whole of *Pride and Prejudice* is conjured up for both in their memory and imagination.

The continuity of the oral tradition, the presentation of known characters in different contexts or different versions of their original, and more particularly the intertext of the known and the new, are always culturally distinctive. Intertext especially is one of the strongest features of English picture books. It contributes to the intriguing nature of these texts, what I have called elsewhere (Meek, 1998) 'secrets' that everyone knows but no one quite explains. Clifford Geertz, the anthropologist, taught me to call this the 'deep play' of reading. Learned early, it constitutes the persistent Englishness of English fiction. English children are subjectively as well as socially located in this literary culture. It is the most difficult thing for outsiders to interpret and it is a great challenge to translators. *Each Peach Pear Plum* exhibits to inexperienced readers how a story 'goes'. It also presents them with a kind of 'multi-consciousness', a simultaneous awareness of a number of things going on at once: seeing, telling, puzzling, understanding, looking. If you ask how I learned about this, I have to say: from Shakespeare. How did *you* come to do it? Have you ever taught a reading child to be aware of this?

I am not suggesting that these features are unique to English children's books. Most literature is the product of language and the imagination. But with the Ahlbergs the semiotic 'thickness' seems richly English. It is interesting to compare Sendak's American-ness in *In the Night Kitchen* with *Peepo!,* another universal game the Ahlbergs turned into a book. The book device is a circle cut out from a page, so that the reader focuses on an object or a person in the following page, then moves into the full scene by turning over, there to find a kitchen, a garden a bedroom, full of the clutter of the early Forties. The implicit story is of a soldier father home on leave from the war, surrounded by his extended family, which includes a baby. Here the Ahlberg partners are responding to the question, asked in this case by their daughter, whose prompts often result in a new picture book, 'What was it like when you were young?'

This reveals another thread in the texture of Englishness, *nostalgia*. Outsiders to the tradition have always maintained that the English, men particularly, recover their childhood by writing about it during their exile in adult life. But the Ahlbergs are not imitating *Peter Pan* – nor *The Wind in the Willows*. What readers know from their first glance at this book with the peepholes in the pages, without a word of explanation, is an entirely different social class from the one most usually represented in children's books of the last century and the early years of this one. The baby in the book is Allan Ahlberg; the house, in all its detail, is where he grew up. The game is 'now you see it, now it's different', a visual ambiguity, like memory. When the page is turned to reveal the panoply of significations of family life, including grandparents, that is history. There's a neat trick near the end. The peephole shows the baby in his mother's arms. His father is wearing his uniform and has his cap on, signifying departure. The page turns, and lo, we are looking into a mirror which shows, in the background behind the baby's head, the baby's bed, at once the guarantee of safety and hope for the future. Janet Ahlberg found the furnishing details for the pictures in an old Army and Navy Stores catalogue she kept because the things illustrated were beautifully engraved. More history. As all displaced readers know, our lives are intertexts; our great concern is to find out where we stand. By reading, whether we are old or young, we get more than one point of view on the past. In this book quite complex social awareness is made available for exploration in the semiotics of the picture text. It is most beautifully done, and the words are so simple, so English English, like lyric poetry, yet entirely without sentimentality.

By the time they produced *The Jolly Postman*, another triumph of book design, the Ahlbergs had taught their readers to expect surprises. In one sense, this book is the sequel to *Each Peach Pear Plum;* in another it is quite different, and very English indeed. As formalities of written communications, letter-writing is always culturally specific. In England's English, letters are also discourse-specific. What is read, besides the words, is the whole lifestyle of the writer as indications of 'manners', the visible forms of class-bound behaviour. The first taboo is: other people's letters are texts out-of-bounds, forbidden by the code of good manners. (There were books in English for children on this topic long before there were storybooks.) In the envelopes that compose the form of the book there are letters, actual instances of literate epistolary practices now current: invitations, apologies, pamphlets, book tokens, advertising fliers, postcards, and letters from lawyers. The story that weaves its way through the book as a text is in verse and lies in the world of the other domain, that of the traditional folktale. Nor is that all. There is an intertext from another series of books for children about a postman.

Adult readers have no difficulty in separating the strands. But they are also compromised because the contents of the letters are about life in the actual here and now. Lawyers write a modern letter to threaten the wicked wolf who is living in Miss Riding Hood's grandmother's cottage and wearing her grandmother's clothes. In a contrite note, Goldilocks apologises to the three bears and invites Baby Bear to her birthday party. Jack, of beanstalk fame, thanks the Giant for international currency derived from the stolen golden eggs. *Alice in Wonderland* has comparable literary jokes, and acts as a kind of godparent to this production in all its intricate subtlety, in that Carroll also took great care of how his book 'worked'. In both books, the readers are invited to be 'in the know' of how readers and writers poach words and ideas from one another.

I suspect that this is not uniquely an English habit. (Barthes says he reads Proust in Stendahl, and Salman Rushdie's story for children, *Haroun and the Sea of Stories* has many hints and references I fail to understand because I am outside the principality of the context they bring with them.) But English life and literature haunts the picture books that English children are at home with. The deliberately polysemic texture devised by book artists comes from the visual semiotics of children's lives, localised as TV and advertising.

The most subtle examples of Ahlberg intertext are in *The Clothes Horse*, a collection of stories I often read with teachers so as to ask them what children have to be able to do to read them. Each title – The Jackpot; Life Savings; The Night Train; The Clothes Horse; God Knows; No Man's Land – is a well-known phrase, a kind of dead metaphor, current in English speech. Here the writer treats each literally and turns it into a narrative. Thus 'Life Savings' becomes the story of an old lady who has saved up part of her *life* (rather than her money, as would be the usual signification), in case she needs it. When she came to be seventy, she 'opened the box with a day in it when she was eight... she rushed out to the park. Here she played on the swings and rolled on the grass and fished in the pond and ate ice cream'. The Jackpot is about a giant who had a pot into which he put all the boys called Jack who came to try to steal his treasure. The Clothes Horse is a horse made of old clothes. My favourite is the Night Train, not the train that goes at night, but the train that brings the night. (For the well-read adult there is also a famous poem of this name by W.H. Auden.) In adult novels these references would be explained in footnotes. Here the writer is counting on the readers' acquaintance with other commonly known stories in English. It is a game for insiders. There is a study of this element of literary writing by Frank Kermode – a famous English critic, who, I imagine, may never have read a picture book for children but who has the perfect description of insider reading. He says readers who are attuned to this cultural verbal play have 'circumsized ears'.

The Ahlbergs are constantly giving their readers the reading lessons they need to grow up in reading. The subtlety is in the interplay of the miniaturisation in the pictures, a kind if statement almost under the breath. The most recent Ahlberg story collection, *The Better Brown Stories* has, sadly, no pictures by Janet. Instead there are dialogic drawings commenting on the prose-tale by the artist, Fritz Wegner, a different kind of intertext in a post-modern narrative. (As yet I have no readings by the young to report on.) In brief, the book begins, like many other stories, with a description of the characters and the setting. Suddenly, the members of the story family express resentment at the ways in which they are characterised and resist the author's treatment of them, demanding that they should appear in quite different stories where they might be differently displayed. To satisfy their demands, the writer, himself a character by this time, inserts them into new versions of well-know stories by 'heritage' authors: Conan Doyle, Stevenson, Somerset Maugham, Raymond, who are in the literary canon prescribed for school reading, and Enid Blyton, who is still a favourite with children, although proscribed by parents and teachers. Thus, the ordinary milkman becomes Jekyll and Hyde: Brian Brown, who demands a story about dogs, becomes Sherlock Holmes on the trail of a modern Hound of the Baskervilles. Mr Brown has the chance for a short time to be Cezanne, *à la mode de* Somerset Maugham. The play of these texts is directed to young adolescents who want to be 'with it' in terms of literary know-how. But the serious business is showing the young the nature of the constructedness of texts, a powerful understanding in an age of media dominance and the need for more general competences in critical literacy.

Here, at last, I think we might see a thinning in the Englishness of English children's books. We might even be becoming European as we watch Allan Ahlberg hook the understanding of Barthes, Genette, Derrida, Eco and others, albeit with his tongue in his cheek from time to time, to the under-standing of children's picture books. Children are quick to spot both readerly and writerly text. They have reading experience of a whole series of narrative kinds, situated perspectives and ways of manoeuvring their way through the post-modern books produced for them to play. They don't know that these narrative differences are deliberate; they simply follow the writer's lead. Adults, on the other hand, expect stories for children to follow classic patterns and are bamboozled when the tale moves away from the sequence of the beginning, middle and end. They need children to show them how to read the texts of the times.

A little coda. When Hazard wrote of the possibility of recreating England from English books for children, he was displaying that Gallic irony that

Stendahl says the French use to avoid the embarrassment of enthusiasm. In Hazard's day, stereotypes were more visible than they are now: over-mannered bourgeois, children abandoned in boarding schools, the stiff upper lip and the rest. These were not the characteristics of English males only. Cezanne and Zola, friends at school in Aix, were displaced persons, although we English think of them as French because we, too, lack the knowledge that brings better understandings and fewer generalisations. We may all have continuing stereotypes of each other, but I think that people are now more sensitive to the nuances of inter-language, and the responses to events that affect us all. But it is certain that the displacement of England, the UK, now in world affairs, has brought about different feelings and perspectives that are changing, even here. It is interesting to see some of this reflected in children's books. Perhaps the Englishness of England that has not been to our advantage will be edited out. Meanwhile, I hope that children's books will continue to encourage aware and critical readers in all countries.

This article first appeared in *European Children's Literature 1,* edited by Penni Cotton and published by Kingston University in 1996. Our thanks to Penni for permission to us it here and for recognising its appropriate new airing.

PART FOUR
Back to the Way Ahead

If, as seems likely, children's literature has as much to do with the readers' dialogues with their future as with their first views of themselves at home, then early encounters with books must make deep impressions. So it seems from the rapidly increasing evidence available from studies of children's attachment to picture books, the art form which joins the history of children's literature with the most recent examples of it. If we are to take seriously the impact of early reading on children's notions of belonging, then picture books will surely help us to see how their views of affiliation, in any sense, are inaugurated. A focused academic interest in how children read pictures now accompanies a thriving international trade in books that make only short (but not small) demands on translators. Picture books are the most transcultural and transnational. International book fairs, publishing deals, prizes and conferences display both the transposition qualities of this material and the nature of its cultural origins. Brian Wildsmith, one of the best-known English originators, has a dedicated art gallery in Japan. Quentin Blake, the British Children's Laureate, is published in France.

As an introduction to a study destined to grow with every new development of book production, Judith Graham considers the Englishness of a selection of picture books by artists whose reputations are worldwide, and whose work has a 'dual address' to parents and children simultaneously. (What could be more English than *The Jolly Postman* or the predominance of class as a social theme?) Like Francis Marcoin, she addresses the complexities that arise from 'other' appearances in the England of a new century. As we near the end of this short study, the way ahead begins to open up.

Penni Cotton has taken several steps forward. She has explored with European colleagues a notion of 'European-ness' which involved the reading in schools of a selection of books from a number of countries in order to determine the ways in which children encounter cultural differences in texts and pictures. Here she surveys what she has learned about the characteristics of literature for the young in terms of language, history and current production and distribution of books. Her main theme is the 'need to make visible all European cultures through literature'. She supports Judith Graham's conviction that picture books are central to this international understanding; the advantage of the picture book is that it transcends speech and written language. Certain 'universal child-hood themes', friendship, for example, 'address contemporary issues'. This *tour d'horizon* serves as a useful view of what lies ahead for those who are willing to take on and extend the theme of this short book, and the concerns of those whose expertise has contributed to it.

The Same or Different:
Children's books show us the way

Judith Graham

In a long career, John Burningham, one of England's most highly regarded children's authors and illustrators, has created picture books for children of great originality and passion. Children continue to be amused, thirty years after its publication, by *Mr. Gumpy's Outing*, in which farmyard animals are punted down an English river by the benign Mr Grumpy who serves tea to them all even though they upset his boat. Shirley's fantasy pirate adventure, played out against an English sea-side, continues to intrigue in *Come Away from the Water, Shirley*, and no-one forgets *Granpa*, which deals tenderly with the relationship between an old man and his granddaugher as he moves towards the end of his life.

In 1992, John Burningham produced the picture book *England*. It was not, however, for children and would probably be of little interest to them. The book represents the nature and culture of England in a completely un-sentimental way, offering us a composite, rich but frequently troubling picture of the country. Through an examination of *England*, I hope to explore concepts of Englishness and 'otherness' (especially in terms of class and race) and then move to selected children's books which offer different images to readers.

England achieves its effects by juxtaposition of images, showing England to be a country of contrast and contradictions, of the occasionally beautiful and the often shameful, of the funny and the sobering. Thus, the proverbial English love of animals is characterised by doughty dog-walkers trying to stay upright in the teeth of a gale along the Brighton sea front, by an image at Crufts (the National annual dog-show) or by much-loved pets on their owners' laps. These views are then mocked by a drawing of cages full of unwanted dogs at Battersea Dogs' Home (the largest animal sanctuary in the country) and views of fox-hunters with their hounds and grouse-shooters with their guns. The sea and the shore figure prominently, positively as the English take tea, play beach cricket, fish or potter in boats, less so as football fans get drunk on a ferry across the channel between England and France.

As well as telling contrasts, Burningham also uses the passing year as a structuring device. He has images of sheep in green fields at the height of summer and motorways blocked by snow in winter. He shows lecherous workmen whistling from their scaffolding at passing girls in springtime; school children on nature trails and Guy Fawkes on his bonfire in autumn. The English are shown as devoted to their seasonal rituals: January sales, Christmas pantomimes or summer flower shows.

Burningham also reveals England as a country where social class is still a great divider. He uses class images of the rich and of the poor as another device to structure his book. Several pages characterise the activities of the upper classes of England, who take their picnic hampers to the opera house at Glyndebourne and tend delphiniums in their stately home gardens. Their effects (oak, mahogany and walnut furniture) are sold at auction rooms. Their elder daughters are featured in the glossy *Country Life* magazine on the occasion of their engagements. Younger offspring are taken by their Norland nannies to the park (Norland' training has great prestige in England), where 'they see nobody they like better than themselves'. Garden parties at Buckingham Palace are accompanied by rules for how to address royalty and, despite the verse which proclaims, 'we must all go a-shooting to-day', it is in fact only the gentry who make up the grouse-shooting party and the gentry whose wills are published in the newspaper. The children of the upper classes are shown shedding tears as they are packed off to private boarding schools at tender ages.

The workers' children also are reluctant on the first day of school, faced with high wire fences and crowded playgrounds, but it is not long before they are joy-riding in stolen cars. Their fathers are shown in their vans, reading the *Sun* (a tabloid newspaper whose readership is predominantly working-class), or whistling at the girls. Mothers and grandmothers smoke and play Bingo in converted cinemas. The dispossessed sleep in cardboard on the pavement, with the Salvation Army brass band keeping their spirits up at Christmas.

Class divisions and, even more, the impact of immigration dominate England. Burningham shows how the country has received arrivals from other countries, both rich and poor. The rich arrive in the form of oil-sheikhs, with six-door, chauffeur-driven limousines and veiled wives, paying for private medicine in Harley Street, London's most expensive medical district. The poor, in Burningham's picture, have taken over the narrow streets and back-to-back houses of the working-class, northern town of Bradford. Superimposed on this picture, Burningham reproduces Bradford's travel guide, still staunchly monocultural. In another pair of pictures, an extract from a 1940 Ministry of Information leaflet entitled *If the Invader Comes*, beginning 'The

Germans threaten to invade England', is followed by a drawing of an old English town at night, characterised by Norman church, cobbled alleys and bow-fronted shops, with a Chinese restaurant the only shop open. Super-imposed on the picture is the Chinese menu. It would be possible to interpret this as the Chinese restaurant offering the only life at night in a sleepy English town but not when the word 'invader' is so recently in our ears. This offers a most troubling conjunction of ideas.

Black faces are few and far between in the book and seldom integrated ex-cept for an uncomfortable couple at a Buckingham Palace garden party, chil-dren in the state school playground, one of the jurors on a British jury (to all of which occasions one could say one is compulsorily summoned) and in a line of prisoners in a jail. Undoubtedly, Burningham feels he is 'telling it like it is', though there are many occasions when black and white mix more voluntarily and enjoyably and still in ways which characterise the nation, such as at the Notting Hill carnival which takes place in London annually over an August week-end.

It is these areas of class and race that I want to reflect upon, as they are clearly key in any nation's sense of itself. That they should also appear in children's picture books, saying something about how we wish things to be, is the focus of the remainder of this piece.

The many and varied ways in which a nation weaves an identity for itself will have been touched on in every piece in this collection. Briefly, a country will retain those aspects of its history which show it in a good light and con-veniently rationalise the others. It will retrieve or perhaps invent myths that embody values and characteristics that it thinks laudable. In the effort to get everybody speaking the same language, and aware of the country's great stories (in the case of England, these might be King Arthur or Robin Hood), it will educate its children in schools and through the media where it can more or less control the content and language of instruction. A nation will have laws that it expects all to obey and institutions that are respected be-cause they are geared to the nation's good. In a sense, the natural pull in any nation is towards homogenising the nation – making everybody as like each other as possible so that, in times of need, all would see the sense of pulling together against an enemy who was 'not like us'.

Elimination of class difference in the UK has frequently been the goal of government, and equality of opportunity has been the declared aim of the school system since the 1944 Education Act. (The continuing private school system might militate against this aim.) But if Burningham's picture of England has any truth in it, and many would say it is accurate, class difference is very visible in the UK. The social classes have little in common and spend their time in vastly different ways and as far as possible with their own kind.

Immigration is in some ways a similar issue. Different races, understandably, especially on arrival in the country, keep together and live together. Although humane laws are passed which give immigrant people rights, and although there is a clear expectation that newcomers deserve respect and freedom to practise and enjoy 'their' culture, this results, at worst, in ghettoisation. This still prevails even though well over half of 'visible' minority people were born here.

So a country where class and race divide people from each other at every turn may not feel a national identity is possible. An event like the accidental death of Princes Diana probably makes the country feel more at one than at any other time but even on that occasion there were large swathes of the nation who dissociated themselves from the communal mourning. The ugly side of patriotism, jingoism – manifest when English footballers play abroad and when an atypical audience arrives to sing patriotic songs and wave Union Jack flags at the last night of the annual Promenade concerts in London, and in many more hidden ways – doesn't help.

The ways in which children's books reflect the nation's tenets and aspirations for itself are inevitably linked to the extent to which writers and illustrators feel part of and imbued with the sense of their country. The quintessentially English pair, Allan and Janet Ahlberg, could not, we feel, have sprung from any other country. But as well as reflecting their country, writers and illustrators have a well-developed sense that they need to create in their child readers ambition and hope that things can be different. It is in children's picture books where we see a possibility of a national identity emerging which is not predicated on division but on friendship and integration. The books tend to reflect the less complicated view of each other that children have, compared with their parents, so to this extent they are realistic whilst also being idealistic, in the long tradition of children's books.

Books which encapsulate hope and ideals appear for the very youngest children. I look here at three picture books which reflect the time when children have to start widening their cultural base most dramatically – when they begin school. All depict school in the UK and all were published in the last quarter of the twentieth century, although, with the changes happening in schools, particularly in early years education, several of the books seem to capture an era recognisable only in memories.

Stories about school, tantalising snippets and full-blown accounts, reach many a pre-school child from older siblings. The siblings have reached that milestone where they leave home and exist all day in a new setting, without their parents. School, as a cultural experience, is often devoutly longed for by the child left at home. This is the scenario Petronella Breinburg and Erroll Lloyd present in *My Brother Sean*. Even on the title page, Lloyd shows us the small Sean sitting at his sister's feet as she reads a book. Sean watches long-ingly through the window at his sister leaves for school, satchel slung over shoulder. But a longed-for experience can be more terrifying in the event than in contemplation. When Sean eventually goes to school, he cries. Mother, sister, teacher and children woo Sean with cuddles, reassurances and references to the various toys, and Sean overcomes his anxiety and joins in with the class activities. Mum and sister slip away.

This is a book of few words but the emotional impact, enhanced by Errol Lloyd's painted illustrations, is considerable. As a child from a black family, Sean has to cross into a world peopled by black children and white. The nursery teacher is black and he finds security there. But the child who offers him his donkey to ride is white. It is he who brings out the 'teeny, weeny smile' in the bashful Sean. *My Brother Sean* was one of the first books pub-lished in the UK which featured black main characters and a multicultural nursery school. It is a book which is powerfully significant for all children, as exemplified by Cushla (in Butler, 1979) who is described solicitously kiss-ing the image of the howling Sean at every reading.

Starting School had its origins in an idea from the first teacher of Allan and Janet Ahlberg's daughter, who wanted to welcome and inform new entrants to school. The Ahlbergs induct readers into the rhythms and rituals of a bliss-ful primary school where the classroom rabbit is allowed to dominate the curriculum for a week, and swimming, baking, painting, dressing-up, model-making, reading *Burglar Bill* (another Ahlberg title) at story-time take their place alongside more formal school work. The particular delight of this book is derived from tracking, in Janet Ahlberg's tiny, detailed illustrations, the individual stories of seven quite different children who start school together. Sushima, for instance, comes to school with her sari-clad mother, leaves her with a cheerful wave and enters eagerly into everything: painting, climbing, swimming and cooking, as much as reading, writing and sums. She finds *Burglar Bill* quietly amusing. She does not put her hands together when a prayer is said in assembly but, later, she readily shows her sari and her Diva lamp. By Christmas time, she seems to be willing to be an angel in the nativity play and her who family comes to the performance. This story is detectable only from close scrutiny of the illustrations; all the children have their own different backgrounds and stories. Their personalities develop over the course of their first term at school. Red-haired Sophie, for instance, develops into a confident and independent child, though she is capable of sniggering in prayers and hurling the odd wooden block and attempting to throttle a classmate. Alternatively, we might watch sturdy black Erroll, whose mother plays the piano at the school and whose father is happy to take the rabbit home for the holidays. The avoidance of stereotypes is commendable and the sense of a multicultural classroom where individuality can flourish and yet where a classroom culture also grows is tangible.

Amazing Grace (Mary Hoffman and Caroline Binch) is a picture book both for and about somewhat older children, and author and illustrator feel able to tackle the issue of race (and of gender) much more directly. The main character, Grace, is a talented girl with a great love of stores and acting. Her class is going to put on a performance of the pantomime, *Peter Pan*, but her classmates tell her that she can't take the main part, not only because, in their ignorance of pantomime traditions, they think that Peter Pan should be played by a boy but also because Peter Pan is not black, as Grace is. (Her mother's roots can be traced back to Trinidad; her father, we discover from a sequel to this book, is from the Gambia.) Grace's grandmother, who has great faith in Grace, takes her to a performance of the ballet Romeo and Juliet, where a black girl dances the main part. Grace is inspired. When the children are auditioned for the play, Grace is everyone's choice and she proves that 'when she puts her mind to it she can do anything'.

In accounting for the phenomenal sales that his book has enjoyed – and not only in the UK – there would have to be mention of the popular theme of 'achievement against the odds' (as well as the book's enormously expressive illustrations), but attention would have to be given also to the overt raising of racist attitudes by Hoffman. In this classroom full of potential tensions, unity, pride and loyalty have been engendered. Classroom culture and therefore culture in its widest sense has been made anew by the children.

Picture books in the UK which tackle the question of the divisions of class in society are rarer than those which show a multicultural society learning to live with itself. Many of the books of the highly respected Charles Keeping centre on working-class characters. *Railway Passage* shows what happens when the occupants of a row of cottages win a large sum of money. Each chooses to spend and use the money in very different ways, revealing Keeping's appreciation of the individuals in a group so frequently assumed to be of one culture. In *Adam and Paradise Island*, his last book, capitalists exploit and potentially ruin a working-class community but ultimately all, particularly the children, show resilience. An earlier title, *Sammy Streetsinger,* has a similar theme: Sammy, who is a one-man band with a local, enthusiastic child following, is taken up by an exploitative entrepreneur and re-packaged as a super-star. Fame is lonely, however, and fleeting, and contentment is only regained when he returns to his roots.

Anthony Browne, another esteemed author/illustrator, through telling juxta-position rather in the Burningham way discussed earlier, has given us two books, more than twenty years apart, which not only comment on class but offer hope. The first title, *A Walk in the Park*, Browne's second book, intro-duces us to Mrs. Smythe, her son Charles and dog Victoria and then to Mr Smith, his daughter Smidge and their dog, Albert. Names, homes, dress, behaviour and language all separate these two households and the separation is underlined if one attends to the surrealist detail in the pictures. But, with the dogs initially showing the way, the children break down the barriers and they, if not their parents, have a great time in the park.

In *Voices in the Park*, the same characters appear but here we have interior monologues from each character. We begin with Mrs. Smythe setting off from her large detached house for the regular walking of their son, Charles, and her pedigree Labrador. She is not happy when a scruffy mongrel lures the dog off to play. She turns her attention to her son, whom she commands to sit, but he also escapes her control. Found eventually, 'talking to a very rough-looking child', both dog and child are walked home in silence.

The rough-looking child is Smudge. The next section of the book is told by her father, who is without work and gloomy. He admires his dog's energy, searches in the newspaper for a job – 'you've got to have a bit of hope haven't you?' – and his mood is greatly improved on the return journey, particularly because of his daughter's cheerful chatter.

The third section is told by Charles, who envies the instant playmate that his dog makes. Gradually, his shyness is overcome and he is drawn, by her friendly overtures, into playing with Smudge. They, like the dogs (and as in the earlier book), become friends, climbing, swinging and sliding together. As he is led from the park, Charles looks back wistfully and hopefully. Cupid, in the form of a statue, aims an arrow at him.

Smudge's voice, chatty and direct in her views, completes the story as she warms to the strange Charles whom, initially, she thought 'a bit of a wimp'. They play, and gradually their play and the dogs' play converge and they cart-wheel together on a huge multi-coloured bandstand. This is the bright, posi-tive climax to the book but there is a quiet coda, as Smudge puts the bright flower that Charlie has given her into a mug delicately decorated with dogs playing in a park.

Every detail in the illustrations, from the cross-hatched shadows that box in poor down-trodden Charles to the glorious life that springs up when Smudge is our guide, suggests that Browne is able through these pictures, to make accessible, some of the complex things that he wants to say about class. Even the typefaces used for each character's monologue are chosen to indicate something of their different outlooks on life.

Picture books such as the ones I have discussed here are not numerous or typical of the output for young children in the UK. Racial and class issues are more likely to be avoided in favour of safer subjects, rather than tackled vigorously as these authors and illustrators do here. But the belief, particularly in these last books of Anthony Browne, that it is through children themselves that solutions will be found to the pressing problems of national conflict, guides the makers of these books, enabling them to write child-friendly books which yet speak of serious things for adults to listen to. In addition, there is, as in many children's books, a valuing of the individual and yet of commonly-held humanity – 'completely different, exactly the same' – which is a good enough basis for any developing conception of national identity.

Books cited

Ahlberg, Allan and Ahlberg, Janet (1988) *Starting School*, London: Viking

Breinburg, Petronella and Lloyd, Errol (1973) *My Brother Sean*, London: The Bodley Head

Browne, Anthony (1977) *A Walk in the Park*, London: Hamish Hamilton

Browne, Anthony (1998) *Voices in the Park*, London: Doubleday

Burningham, John (1992) *England*, London: Jonathan Cape

Burningham, John (1998) *France*, London: Jonathan Cape

Burningham, John (1970) *Mr Gumpy's Outing*, London: Jonathan Cape

Burningham, John (1977) *Come Away from the Water, Shirley*, London: Jonathan Cape

Burningham, John (1984) *Granpa*, London: Jonathan Cape

Butler, Dorothy (1979) *Cushla and her Books*, London: Hodder and Stoughton

Hoffman, Mary and Binch, Caroline (1991) *Amazing Grace*, London: Frances Lincoln

Keeping, Charles (1974) *Railway Passage*, Oxford University Press

Keeping, Charles (1984) *Sammy Streetsinger*, Oxford: Oxford University Press

Keeping, Charles (1989) *Adam and Paradise Island*, Oxford: Oxford University Press

The Europeaness of Picture Books

Penni Cotton

Colm Tóibín, the Irish writer, discussing his current novel which was short-listed for the Booker Prize, said he wanted to create 'a world around that which you couldn't really call Ireland and didn't really have any history and didn't really have any politics in it'. He suggested that he was trying to write a play about contemporary universal family issues that are likely to arise in Ireland, rather than a more traditional work related to historical developments in his native country. Many of his critics, however, believe that *The Blackwater Lightship* is a deeply political novel and that the whole family could be a metaphor for Ireland struggling to come to terms with its history.

Is it possible to gain insights into cultures without probing the depths of histories and ideologies, and how might our perceptions of who we are, either nationally or within Europe, be influenced by this insight? Tóibín's concern, to show Ireland as a country whose current social issues also permeate other cultures, reflects the aspirations of other European writers. Throughout the continent, people in most countries wish to share beliefs and values through their literature for adults and children. Perhaps we should be asking ourselves if it is feasible to address universal contemporary issues in the stories we tell our children, without implicit reference to the historical features which have contributed to shaping identities. I should like to consider the possibility of using universal *childhood* themes, such as friendship or family conflict, in helping children to identify with their European neighbours and thus gain a sense of Europeaness.

Since 1996, I have had the opportunity to draw on the knowledge and expertise of many European colleagues working in the field of children's literature, some of whom have contributed to this volume (Cotton, 1996; 1998). In recent years, we have been sharing our ideas and exploring the notion of Europeaness through children's literature, focusing particularly on picture books. Here, I draw on some personal reflections of literature and cultural identity, and try to suggest ways in which future generations of children might be helped to acknowledge their own national identities, yet understand what it means to be European.

When looking at the development of European children's literature during the twentieth century, one sees how historical events have influenced the style and content of children's books throughout the continent. For example, many countries have experienced political totalitarianism, which has affected both the content and the actual production of the books.

The most westerly European country, Portugal, has experienced much political repression, which has had an effect on children's literature. At the beginning of the century, leading political figures openly encouraged reading and acclaimed publications such as Ana de Castro's *Para Crianças (For Children)*. The governmental changes of the 1930s began to restrict freedom of speech and education was seen as politically dangerous; compulsory schooling was reduced to three years and very few books were published. During the 1940s, ideology affected literary themes and governmental publications such as *Mocidade Portuguesa (Portuguese Youth)* predominated. These newspapers and magazines focused on well-behaved and submissive children. For the regime, humility was the supreme virtue and literature was seen as subversive (Vila Maior, 1996: 110). Political censorship between 1930 and 1970 made it difficult to produce books in Portugal in which young readers could identify themselves as having a sense of national belonging. It was not until the 1970s that children's books began to reflect the real world of childhood and include humour. In 1974, censorship was abolished and previously taboo subjects were included in children's books through the use of realism, allegory and metaphor. During this period, books like *O Veado Florido (The Flourishing Red Deer)*, an allegory about lost and found freedom, began to appear. Characters, events and settings in stories for children now reflect current social conditions as well as historic and anticipated changes.

In Germany, situated more centrally within Europe, social changes in the 1980s such as techno-militaristic dangers and ecological issues presented a challenge for children's literature. Michael Ende's *Kinder von Schewenborn* and Gudrun Pausewang's *Die Wolke* reflect these issues but espouse contradictory political viewpoints. Whereas Ende favours the 'inner journey to win new consciousness', Pausewang suggests one should act politically and not passively accept political decisions. In 1989, the unification of East and West Germany began a period when literature could, on the one hand, help to overcome the difficulties of a new, different life but, on the other, could be a reminder of the past (Kaminsky, 1996: 31) An important group of writers from the former GDR succeeded in establishing itself on the German literary scene, thus influencing both the content and the style of the country's literature. Kirsten Boie's *Ich Ganz Cool*, for example, uses the 'street-wise' language of a ten year old boy to convey the underlying contemporary German scene.

The dramatic historical changes which took place in Germany and, more easterly, in Hungary have improved relationships between the two countries. Hungarian books have in the past portrayed the stereotypical German in many guises – the troublemaker, intriguer, figure of ridicule, comic enemy or generous friend. Just after the second World War, it was not unusual to see a shouting, paranoid Nazi soldier contrasted with a smiling Russian distributing bread to the starving children of Budapest, as examples of social realism in children's literature (Adamik-Jászó, 1998: 97). Before the unification of Germany, Hungarian children's literature was heavily influenced by the political oppression that dominated the 1950s. Mostly paralleling Soviet directives, books such as *Majd a Gyerekek (The Children Will Do It)* by László Hárs followed this pattern. Currently, one of the main goals of literature in Hungary is to educate children towards tolerance and mutual understanding of other people and cultures. In *The New Landlord* Mór Jókai emphasises the need to overcome prejudices that are generated from bitter historical experiences.

Although neighbouring Croatia also had to march to the tune of the anti-Fascist movement following World War Two, the war of the '90s shook the very roots of Croation society (Javor, 1998: 53). This is reflected in current publications for children which address the issues of war through both prose and poetry. Due to the restrictions on publishing, this material is mainly accessible through magazines such as *Smib, Radost* and *Modra Lasta*. Bosnian children's literature production has suffered a similar fate, with the additional problem that writers in the Bosnian, Croat or Serb languages all had to be represented in the country's literature for young people (Sarajlic, 1998: 47). Further east in Romania, which has its own publishing problems, well-known artists have been recording classic Romanian tales onto audio cassettes. This has provided children with some access to the work of Romania's classical storytellers like Ion Creanga. Unfortunately, as in many other European countries, native literature is poorly represented and is being stifled by foreign books in translation (Stefanescu, 1998: 68).

Native literature, according to Fernandez (1996: 120), is rarely available in Spain. He suggests that as there are so many translated children's books available, very few are written by Spanish writers and references to Spanish culture are sparse. Conversely, UK children have little access to contemporary literature from other countries. The Portuguese suggest that foreign children's literature predominates in their country because it is cheaper to buy from abroad than to pay their own authors. Spaniards, who receive about 44% of their children's books in translation, believe that 'everything coming from abroad is better' (Fernandez, 1996: 120). The reverse seems to be the case in the UK – a belief that British is best. One wonders whether this is an indication that our sense of national identity is more secure, or simply that we are unwilling to venture into other contemporary literary worlds or, even more likely, that translated books are not economically viable.

The Netherlands includes a variety of books from other cultures in its canon of children's literature, yet also has a large number of 'home grown' children's authors such as Dick Bruna. In addition, Dutch readers share a linguistic and literary heritage with the Flemish-speaking part of Belgium. Since the early 1950s, the climate for Dutch children's books has been a friendly and fruitful one, due to 'economic developments and the liberal attitude towards young people' (Boonstra, 1998: 33). A small subsidy is given annually to publishers for the creation of innovative picture books. Defourny (1996: 3) praises these publications and believes that if they remain confined to the Netherlands, it will be a loss for the rest of Europe. He suggests that an original childhood culture has been emerging in the Netherlands since the seventeenth century which is well expressed in present day children's literature; particularly in the books of Katrien Holland, Hariot van Reek, Imme Drosse and Harrie Geelan.

Flemish children's literature does not have a long history, because of the political cultural and linguistic search for a Flemish identity after the artificial creation of the Belgian State in 1830 (Leysen, 1998: 29). In the nineteenth century, the dominance of the French language in Belgium inhibited the growth of reading in Dutch; the Flemings were poor and subservient and despised by the more cultured French speakers. The situation changed around the beginning of the twentieth century when, as a result of the Flemish Movement, the Flemings were given a fresh start. Matters continued to improve, especially during the 1950s, when a new generation of authors of strip cartoons, such as Hergé (*Tintin*), became internationally famous. Currently, about 100 new Flemish children's books are published each year and distributed throughout Flanders. Flemish picture book illustrators such as Lieve Baeten, Ingid Godon and Klaas Verplancke have the ability to tell stories that are universally understood.

Until relatively recently Gaelic (Irish) was also perceived as a language of poverty and economic powerlessness (Flanagan, 1996: 33). At the beginning of the twentieth century a number of individuals who dominated cultural, literary and political life, such as P.H. Pearse, W.B. Yeats, James Larkin, Sean O'Casey and James Stephens, used their interest in Irish language and literature to develop radical educational policies. Pearse's ambition, for example, was to write in the language of the people who spoke the language rather than in the language of those who studied it. From then on, children's books began to look to the traditions, experience and language of the rural Irish-speaking community for their inspiration and expression. Currently, a revival of interest in the Irish language has meant that the publication of books in Irish is becoming more commercially viable as well as culturally acceptable.

Linguistic identity for some European countries is complex and is influenced by their position within the continent. Switzerland has tended to absorb the surrounding cultures and meld them into what today is defined as its national autonomy (Von Stockar, 1996: 91). For the Swiss to develop a cultural self-understanding, they have needed to study the tensions between openness towards the world and a self-centred attitude of withdrawal. The state territory of Switzerland embraces four different language areas: Swiss-German, French, Italian and Rumantsch, each influenced by the neighbouring cultural literatures of the same language, rather than of Switzerland as a whole. A child from the French or Italian part of Switzerland reads entirely different books from a Swiss German child. For example, the much admired Swiss-French children's illustrator Etienne Delessert has created many highly acclaimed picture books but his readership is mainly French and Swiss-French.

The situation in Luxembourg is even more diverse. Only about 70% of children have Luxembourgish nationality; the remainder are Portuguese, Italian, French, Belgian and German. Although there has been a revival of Luxembourgish language and literature since 1986, children usually learn to read in a foreign language. A new children's writer has been creating contemporary literature in Luxembourgish, to promote the country's mother tongue. Guy Rewenig focuses on the linguistic situation in Luxembourg today, and tries to show that people demonstrate the class of society to which they belong through language (Sahr, 1996: 107). The popularity of his *Kätt Trilogy*, which focuses on the everyday antics of a young Luxembourgish girl, is just one example of his publications which are currently read by about 80% of the population, both adults and children.

The linguistic diversity in both Luxembourg and Switzerland demonstrates the role that language plays in giving young children access to social values and cultural codes. The implication is that if countries have similar linguistic codes, they are more likely to absorb each other's culture through the literature that is available to them. The geographical proximity of many Northern European countries often allows for comprehension between languages and literatures. In the Polar Regions of Norway, Sweden, Finland and Russia the 100,000 inhabitants all share the Sami language, and children's books are now being published for them. Historically, the language and literature of the Nordic countries have varied considerably, as a result of changing political boundaries. The search for Finnish identity, for example, has influenced the literary canon for children. Finland became independent from Russia only in 1917, having been part of Sweden for several hundred years; this has greatly affected its political, cultural and linguistic identity. Linguistically, Finland is a country divided. Although most Finns speak Finnish, many of those living in the populated South speak Swedish as their first language. This is the case with Tove Janssen, creator of the internationally known *Moomins*; she publishes in Swedish and is translated into many other languages, including Finnish.

If there is such a thing as a *leitmotif* in Central European children's literature, Sollat (1998:25) suggests that in Austrian picture books it has been the artist's dedication to the weaker members of society, to the 'outsiders'. The idea of peace and tolerance can be found over and over again, for all groups and within all genres and styles. *Das Land der Ecken (The Land of Corners)* suggests in its simplicity a possible harmony, within the differences that exist, and could be seen as a metaphor for friendship across contemporary Europe. Polish children's books express the changes in everyday life, customs and culture. *Five Millions in Cash*, by Edmund Niziurski, in which primary school children decide to start their own business enterprise, ironically reflects the re-birth of capitalism in Poland. (Zajac, 1998: 62).

In Slovakia, modern fantasy tales differ from the traditional line in that the authors bring new elements into children's literature – a bit of subversiveness that was badly needed, fresh topics and novel themes (Prelotzniková, 1998: 74). In Ján Mileák's *Chlapapec Lampásik (The Little Boy Sparky)*, an artist paints a picture on the white wall of a house. As he tells the story, so he adds to the picture. The universal theme of conflict is portrayed, as the parents criticise this 'graffiti' while the children and the artist perceive the world with their hearts rather than their eyes. Books such as this often contain criticisms of present day realities, and are loved by children if not by adults. Slovenia also produces much literature for children which focuses on contemporary life and this, suggests Saksida (1998: 80), is one of the 'mechanisms of culture'. Children's literature today is characterised by the prevalence of visual imagery where focus is placed on the more serious aspects of life, unhappy and uncertain periods as well as the good times, as depicted in Francic's *Otrostvo (Childhood)*, dealing with themes such as hatred, horror and a mother's death.

Today, through universal themes, children's books from many parts of Europe reflect a society with disruption and ambiguity. The difference between the child's world and the adult's is not as clear as it was fifty years ago. In some countries, the image of the father seems to have taken on a more direct domestic role, especially in France (Marcoin, 1996: 30), where the child often has to take on a parent's responsibility, thus bringing out his inner resources. The theme of C.K. Duboic' *Un Papa d'Aventure* is one of assuming a parent's role: a young boy has to face darkness and fear while his father sleeps. This is perhaps an indication that young people in Europe are now more accepting of change and how to cope with it.

Children's fiction, suggests Stephens (1992:8), 'belongs firmly within the domain of cultural practices which exist for the purpose of socialising their target audience'. Now that the world of most European children is beginning to expand beyond a single national identity, it could be argued that there is a need to make visible all European cultures through literature. Unfortunately, the language barrier and the dearth of translated texts renders these narratives inaccessible to many young Europeans.

Although language has such an important role to play in transmitting cultural knowledge and ideologies, it is difficult for Europeans to experience a sense of mutual belonging solely through the spoken word. The use of visual images in picture books helps cultural understanding to transcend the limitations of speech. Von Stockar's belief (1996:96) is that the picture book is in a privileged position, as the visual images surmount the boundaries of language and culture.

It is perhaps through the visual narratives of European picture books that children might gain a sense of what it means to be European. Poesio (1998: 107), suggests that the evaluative skills of young readers in image analysis constitute a sort of mental and cultural common denominator that promotes mutual understanding. The extent of this commonality depends on appreciation of diverse aspects of the images. Through the creative power of the artist, the young reader is made aware of the universality of social, political and cultural problems beyond geographical boundaries. In the internationally renowned picture book *Rosa Bianca*, a young girl experiences the horrors of World War Two. Author Roberto Innocenti allows his readers to become emotionally involved in her plight, through the changing colours and hues of his illustrations which underscore the development of the story far more effectively than words. Poesio's thinking endorses Stephens' (1992: 158) comment that 'picture books can never be said to exist without either a socialising or educational intention, or else without a specific orientation towards the reality constructed by the society that produces them'.

The picture books which are most likely to transcend national boundaries are those which focus on universal childhood themes. Many of these have been included in a European collection of picture books (Cotton, 2000) that has been created with funding from the European Union. It is through focusing on similarities between nations that young children are able to empathise with each other. If the universal themes are embedded within visual settings which make cultural references to each country, a natural pathway towards greater European understanding evolves. The story of loss and friendship in *El Guardian del Olivido*, set in the arid-brown landscape of Spain and paying homage to Salvador Dali, exemplifies this.

The naturalistic theme, prevalent in the Swedish picture books of Elsa Beskow, appears frequently in the literature of many northern European countries. In Estonia, Edgar Valter pursues an iconotextual approach of his work, where his characters are at one with nature (Müürsepp, 1998: 60). Denmark's typical landscape – trees, lakes, animals and beautiful sunsets – all feature in *Mosekonens Bryg (The Old Woman of the Marsh)* (Trondhjem, 1998: 39). The role of the sea in Finland and its effect on individuals is discussed by Kjellman (1998: 14). She points out that literary characters who are wary of the unfamiliar reflect the personality of many Finns, rather like the protagonist in *Ven Ska Trösta Knyttet (Who Will Comfort Toffle?)*. She also stresses the significance of folktales told through picture books, and the tradition of storytelling when the nights grow long in winter.

In much Scandinavian literature, children are allowed to be themselves and are free from the responsibilities that belong to the adult world. This is in stark contrast to *Katie Morag and the New Pier*, from Scotland, where the eponymous Katie helps her Granny to cope with life's changes (Hill, 1996: 139). Here the responsibility on the shoulders of the young protagonist is much greater than in stories from Nordic countries. This may bear some relationship to the variation in the age at which children begin school. In most Scandinavian countries they start around the age of seven, when formal reading instruction begins; whereas in the UK it is five, as depicted in *Starting School*, where the Ahlbergs 'offer smaller, infinitely revealing vistas of English social life' (Meek, 1996: 148).

Addressing contemporary issues appears to be the main role of European children's literature at the end of the twentieth Century. Writers/illustrators of picture books reflect Colm Tóibín's literary aims as they want to create worlds which reflect the cultures of today that 'don't really have any history or any politics in them'. Unfortunately, like Tóibín's critics, readers of these books may draw parallels with past events, using the visual representations as a metaphor for cultural identity. Dunbar (1996: 44) in fact suggests that many Irish writers for both adults and children have long been drawn to the dark as a metaphor for their psychological and emotional self-examination, particularly in the recesses of their distant childhood. In contrast, Marriott (1998: 124) believes that a perspective on moral and ethical values provided through picture books can constructively reflect the author's aspirations for the present and future nature of society.

In the Greek story *Tin-City*, it is the way in which author A. Fakinou arranges the relationships between the tin cans and how the reader responds to this, which creates the reading experience characteristic of the picture book genre. Written in 1977, just after the seven-year military dictatorship ended, this visual narrative could be seen as a metaphor for the political problems of that time. In the story, a group of small tins are living harmoniously, until an over-sized neighbour begins to dominate their existence. Finally, they gang up against him with tin openers, cut him to pieces, then revert to their previous lives. As an example of childhood conflict, young children are likely to accept this story at face value. Alerting more experienced readers to the underlying socio-political histories implicit within the text will facilitate the aculturalisation process. For as Manna (1997: 150) says, literature constitutes 'a shared way of interpreting the world'; it teaches children to perceive the world in terms which unite groups within and across cultures, basic human needs, drives and conflicts.

A sense of Europeaness is a much more achievable goal than a quest for European identity. It implies that as Europeans we need to feel for ourselves what it is like to be European; to believe in our own national identities yet acknowledge the similarities and celebrate the cultural variances that exit between us. Cummings (1997: 34) suggests that familiarity with other cultures can bring about an understanding of them, and that 'respect is not such a great distance from understanding'. My colleagues and I hope that, through sensitive discussion of the visual narratives in carefully selected picture books, it will be possible to help our children to live more harmoniously and respect each other.

Works cited

Boonstra, B. (1998) 'Some Thoughts on Dutch Picture Books' in P. Cotton, *European Children's Literature II*, Kinston: Kingston University.

Cotton, P. (1996) *European Children's Literature I*, Kingston: Kingston University.

Cotton, P. (1998) *European Children's Literature II*, Kingston: Kingston University.

Cotton, P. (1999a) 'Picture Books: A European Perspective', in *Journal of Children's Literature*, vol. 25, no. 1: 18-27, Spring 1999.

Cotton, P. (1999b) 'The European Picture Book Collection' in *Children's Literature in Education*, vol. 30, no. 2: 45-56, Autumn, 1999.

Cotton, P. (2000) *Picture Books Sans Frontières*, London: Trentham.

Cummings, P. (1997) 'Global Visual' in Manna, A.L. and Brodie, C.S., *Art & Story: The Role of Illustration in Multicultural Literature for Youth*, Wisconsin: Highsmith Press.

Defourny, M. (1966) 'Contribution for a Better Understanding of Children's Literature in Europe', in Cotton *op cit.*

Dunbar, R. (1996) 'Children's Literature in The Republic of Ireland', in Cotton *op cit.*

Fernandez, J.J. (1996) 'The Situation of Children's Literature and the Promotion of Reading Activities in Spain', in Cotton *op cit.*

Flanagan, F. (1996) 'Children's Literature in the Republic of Ireland', in Cotton *op cit.*

Hill, A. (1996) 'Talking About Reading in Scotland', in Cotton *op cit.*

Javor, R. (1998) 'Croatian Children's Literature', in Cotton *op cit.*

Kaminski, W. (1996) 'Two Concepts of Children's Literature from a German Point of View', in Cotton *op cit.*

Kåreland, L. (1996) 'Swedish Children's Literature: An Historical Perspective and Recent Trends', in Cotton *op cit.*

Leysen, A. (1998) 'Children's Books in Flanders: An Historical Introduction', in Cotton *op cit.*

Manna, A.L. (1997) 'About the Virginia Hamilton Conference' in Manna, A.L. and Brodie, C.S., *Art & Story: The Role of Illustration in Multicultural Literature for Youth*, Wisconsin: Highsmith Press.

Marriott, S. (1998) 'Picture Books and the Moral Imperative', in Cotton *op cit.*

Müürsepp, M. (1998) 'A Short Overview of Illustrations in Estonian Children's Books', in Cotton *op cit.*

Poesio, C. (1998) 'The Many Gates of the Picture Book', in Cotton *op cit.*

Sahr, R. (1996) 'Language, Children's Literature and Reading in Luxembourg', in Cotton *op cit.*

Saksida, I. (1998) 'How Childhood is Understood and Presented in Contemporary Slovene Literature', in Cotton *op cit.*

Sarajlic, M. (1998) 'Publishing in Bosnia and Herzegowina: Before and after the War', in Cotton *op cit.*

Sollat, K. (1998) 'Contemporary Picture Books in Austria', in Cotton *op cit.*

Stefanescu, D. (1998) 'Children's Literature in Romania: Between Despair and Hope', in Cotton *op cit.*

Stephens, J. (1992) *Language and Ideology in Children's Fiction*, London: Longman

Trondhjem, K. (1998) 'Examples of Danish Picture Books', in Cotton *op cit.*

Vila Maior, I. (1996) 'Children's Literature in Portugal: A Brief Outline', in Cotton *op cit.*

Von Stockar, D. (1996) 'Swiss Picture Books in Universal, European and Regional Colours', in Cotton *op cit.*

Zajac, M. (1998) 'Polish Children's Literature in the Period of Transition', in Cotton *op cit.*

Afterword

We can rarely tell in advance how the books young people read might influence them. Many a serious writer has confessed to an adolescent addiction to popular series fiction deplored by parents. Text details, especially in picture books, may linger in the reader's memory when the carefully inserted information has been assimilated or forgotten. Stories may come back to us as feelings related to the total reading experience even if the sequence of the events is no longer clear. There is some evidence that folk and fairy tales survive as reworked understandings of early reading encounters.

In books where the words and the pictures enhance and extend each other, the cultural details enrich the readers' understanding without having to be emphasised. For example, Shirley Hughes' picture storybook, *The Lion and the Unicorn*, depicts the burning of east London in the blitz, from which Lenny Levi is evacuated to a grand house in the country. His link with home is the lion and unicorn badge his father gave him before he went off to the army. Lenny's troubles, bedwetting, being afraid of strange noises at night, excused from school prayers, jeered at and missing his parents, are overlaid with the visual details, first of London on fire, then countryside and the ancestry of Mick, the war hero with one leg missing, who lives in the house but doesn't eat his meals in the kitchen. All the signs of the English class system are there to be read, including an earlier children's book:

> There was a summerhouse half hidden in ivy and beyond it, set in a high stone wall, a wooden door. It was not the door to somebody's house, Lenny knew that. It was a garden door He remembered hearing somewhere about a secret garden that was locked up for years and years and nobody went in.

Adults see and read the embedded specific national identity, but the author-artist moves beyond the obvious signs. Lenny's badge is the transitional object that gives him courage. Mick explains that the courageous are often frightened. Lenny tells Mick his father is 'fighting the Germans like you did'.

> 'I never wanted to fight the Germans or anyone else', Mick told him. 'It's cruelty, bullying and oppression we're fighting against.' Lenny was not quite sure what this meant but he got the general idea.' (Hughes, 1998)

'Getting the general idea' of most things represented by abstract nouns is perhaps one of the ways children come to know what constitutes national identity as 'the usual'. The harder puzzle for readers is how to shift to another point of view from the one they have learned to take for granted. Edward Said (1993) offers this: 'all cultures are involved in one another, none is single and pure, all are hybrid, heterogeneous, extraordinarily differentiated and unmonolithic'.

The writers in this book have different starting points, different examples and perspectives of the common topic. They all have some responsibility for what children read, from the early stages to the end of compulsory schooling. Some are more global in their interests than others. But there is no doubt about their common conviction that narrative is at the heart of children's world-making. In the wake of runaway publishing success, adults have come to be convinced that if the details, conventions and literary archetypes are universal, so are the children's problems. It is childhood, rather than any weakening of local culture that will bring the next generations of the young to European-ness. We need still more involvement in one another.

This book will have served its purpose if it brings to the fore the relevance of children's literature to understanding the nature of 'a sense' of national identity. Clearly, it is something we need to think more about, differently.

List of Contributors

Anna Adamik-Jászó received her PhD at the Department of Hungarian Linguistics and is now Chair at Eotvos Lorand University, Budapest (Faculty of Teacher Training). Her main publications are: *The History of Hungarian Reading Instruction* (1990), *The Book of Hungarian Language* (1991) and the *History of Reading and Writing in Pictures* (1999). Recently she co-ordinated and partly wrote a new programme for grades 1-2: *Integrated Hungarian Language and Literature*. She is also editor of the journal *Magyartanitas* (Teaching Hungarian) She was a Fulbright Scholar and a visiting professor in the USA, where she taught comparative children's literature and the psychology of reading.

Anthea Bell was educated at Somerville College, Oxford and lives in Cambridge. She has worked as a translator for many years, primarily from German and French. Her translations include works of non-fiction (biography, politics social history and musicology), literary and popular fiction and numerous children's books, including classic German works by the Grimm Brothers, Clemens Brentano, Wilhelm Hauff and Christian Morgenstern. She has received many prizes and awards, including the Mildred Batchelder Award in 1979, 1990 and 1995; the 1987 Schlegel-Tieck Prize for Hans Bemman's *The Stone and the Flute*; and in 1996 the first Marsh Award for Children's Literature in Translation for Christine Nostlinger's *A Dog's Life*. Anthea Bell has also served on the committee of the Translators' Association and the jury panel of the Schlegel Tieck German translation prize in the UK.

Penni Cotton is the author of *Picture Books Sans Frontiéres* (Trentham), which draws on the work she has pioneered in promoting a wider European perspective on children's picture books by bringing together a group of researchers from a number of European countries. In 1997 she received the International Reading Association Award for Innovative Reading Promotion in Europe. Her work on 'Common Themes in European Children's Literature' has been widely recognised. She is now a senior lecturer at the National Centre for Research in Children's Literature at Roehampton Institute of Education, the University of Surrey.

Robert Dunbar is the lecturer in charge of English at the Church of Ireland College of Education, Dublin. Additionally, he teaches courses in children's literature at Trinity College, Dublin, and at St Patrick's College, Dublin City University. He has lectured in Ireland and abroad on many aspects of children's literature and is a regular reviewer of children's books in a wide range of publications He was a founder member and twice president of the Children's Literature Association of Ireland and he edited the first fifteen issues of the Association's magazine, *Children's Books in Ireland*. He has edited *First Times, Enchanted Journeys: Fifty Years of Irish Writing for Children, Secret Lands: The World of*

Patricia Lynch, and, with Gabriel Fitzmaurice, *Rusty Nails and Astronauts*, an anthology of poetry for children.

Carol Fox is Reader in Education at the University of Brighton. *At the Very Edge of the Forest*, her distinctive and important study of the narratives of pre-school children who had books and stories read aloud to them, marked a turning point in the understanding of language development and of the influence of children's literature on children before they learn to read. She has been a guest lecturer at the University of Witwatersrand in Johannesburg. The Comenius research project, a collaboration with partners from Belgium and Portugal, resulted in a trilingual annotated bibliography of children's literature about war. She also reviews children's books for the *Times Literary Supplement*, supervises research students and is co-editor of *Challenging Ways of Knowing; in English, Mathematics and Science*. (Falmer Press, 1996)

Judith Graham was teaching in a London secondary school when she co-authored *Achieving Literacy* with Margaret Meek in 1983. Thereafter she taught at the Institute of Education and the University of Greenwich. She now shares her teaching between the Education faculty at the University of Surrey, Roehampton and the School of Education at the University of Cambridge. Her particular interest in illustration-text relations in children's books is the subject of many articles that have followed her books, published by the National Association for the Teaching of English: *Pictures on the Page* (1990), *Cracking Good Books* (1997) and *Cracking Good Picture Books* (1999). With Alison Kelly she has written *Reading under Control* and *Writing under Control*.(David Fulton, 1997, 1998)

Gillian Lathey was for many years happily employed as a teacher in an infants' school in north London before joining the Education faculty at the University of Surrey, Roehampton, where she is currently Deputy Director of the National Centre for Research in Children's Literature. She has a particular (PhD) interest in translation and the variety of ways in which children's literature crosses cultural and linguistic boundaries. She also convenes the judges for the Marsh Award for Children's Literature in Translation.

Francis Marcoin is Professor of French Literature at the University of Artois in Arras. His specialist interest is in fiction, particularly that written for children. He is the author of *A l'ecole de la litterature* and of *La Comtesse de Segur ou le bonheur immobile*. In addition, he is the Director of *Les Cahiers Robinson*, a magazine devoted to childhood and children's reading.

Margaret Meek Spencer is Reader Emeritus at the Institute of Education in the University of London She is the author of *Learning to Read* (1982), *How Texts Teach What Children Learn* (1988), *On Being Literate* (1991), *Information and Book Learning*, (1996) and the editor of various collections of writings about children's literature and reading, including *The Cool Web* (1977). She was awarded the Eleanor Farjeon Prize for services to children's literature, which included being on the jury for the Kurt Maschler (Emil) Award. The National Literacy Trust, the Foundation for Language in Primary Education and IEDPE engage her interests on their boards and committees.

Morag Styles has lectured internationally on the teaching of literature, literacy and, particularly, poetry. At Homerton College, Cambridge, where she is Reader in Children's Literature and Language, she has been responsible for a series of scholarly colloquia which have resulted in important publications on diverse topics related to children's literature: *After Alice* (1992), *The Prose and the Passion* (1994) and *Voices Off* (1996). She is the initiator and responsible for the millennium symposium on *Reading Pictures: Art, Narrative and Childhood,* held in collaboration with the Fitzwilliam Museum

Emer O'Sullivan teaches and carries out her research in the Johann Wolfgang Goethe Research Institute in Frankfurt. Born in Ireland, she has the advantages of bilingual and multi-cultural interests in both English and German. With her husband, she has produced books that encourage children's reading in these two languages. She has explored in depth the aesthetic potential of national stereotypes in children's literature after 1960. *Friend and Foe: The Image of Germany and the Germans in British children's literature from 1870 till the present* offers a more balanced perspective than others on a vital topic. Her complex study of comparative research in children's literature encourages readers to avoid the simplification of issues such a national identity, for the sake of better understanding of diversity and difference.

Carla Poesio, a former high school teacher, was appointed by the Italian Ministry of Education to be a researcher with special responsibility for the promotion of reading, in the National Institute of Pedagogics. Subsequently, she went to the Ministry of Foreign Affairs as coordinator for the promotion of reading in Italian communities abroad. Since 1981 she has been a freelance consultant for in-service courses for teachers and librarians who are concerned to update their studies of books for young people, and also for the Bologna Book Fair. Other teaching commitments have taken her to the University of Ferrara as a specialist in children's literature. Her present concerns include contributions to specialised journals and she is a member of a jury for national and international competitions. She has also written non-fiction books for children and young people, and translated into Italian books from French and English.

Bibliography

Anderson, B. (1983) *Imagined Communities; reflections on the origin and spread of nationalism*. London: Verso (new ed)

Batho, R., Leysen, A. De Wynck, A., Fox, C., Gutterez, R., Fonselo, M. (1998) *War and Peace in Children's Books: a selection* (English, Dutch, Portuguese) obtainable from Carol Fox, Faculty of Education, University of Brighton BN1 9PH

Benton, M. (196) 'Reader response Critics', in *The International Companion Encyclopedia of Children's Literature* ed. P. Hunt. London: Routledge

Boland, E. (1996) *Object Lessons*. London: Vintage

Butler, D. (1979) *Cushla and her Books*. London: Hodder and Stoughton

Chaudhuri, A. (2000) *The New World*. London: Picador

Department of Education and Employment (1995) *English in the National Curriculum*. London: HMSO

Donghi, B.S. (1993) *La Fiabba Come Racconto*. Florence: Mondadori

Eagleton, T. (2000) *The Idea of Culture*. Oxford: Blackwell

Elkin, J. (1985) *A Multicultural Guide to Children's Books*. London: Books for Keeps

Fox, C., Laysen, A. and Koender, S. *In Times of War: an anthology of war and peace in children's literature*. London: Pavilion Books

Gellner, E. (1977) *Nationalism*. London: Weidenfeld and Nicholson

Giddens, A. (1991) *The Consequences of Modernity*. Cambridge: Polity Press

Green, R.L. (ed) *The Diaries of Lewis Carroll*. London, Cassell

Hazard, P. (1932) *Books, Children and Men*. Boston: The Horn book

Heaney, S. (1995) *The Redress of Poetry*. London: Faber

Imperial War Museum (1989) *Scrapbook*. London: HMSO

Ishiguro, K. (1989) *The Remains of the Day*. London: Faber

Jászó, A. (1998) The magician strategy in Hungary. In *The Moonmins in the World – learning with text*. ed. K. Sarnavouri, Turku, University of Turku

Josipovici, G. (1999) *On Trust; Art and the Temptations of Suspicion*. New Haven: Yale University Press

Keating, P.J. (1971) *The Working Classes in Victorian Fiction*. London, Routledge

Keenan, C. (1996) 'Irish Historical Fiction' in *The Big Guide to Irish Children's Books*. ed. V. Coghlan and C. Kennan. Dublin: Irish Children's Book Trust

Kermode, F. (1979) *The Genetics of Secrecy*. Cambridge Mass.: Harvard University Press

Kiberd, D. (1995) *Inventing Ireland*. London: Cape

Kirkpatrick, D. ed (1978) *Twentieth Century Children's Writers*. London: St James Press; subsequent editions 1985, 1989, 1995

Lathey, G. (1999) 'Other sides of the Story: war in translated children's fiction. *Signal 88*. Stroud: The Thimble Press

Meek, M. (1988) *How Texts Teach What Readers Learn*. Stroud: Thimble Press

Nicolayeva, M. (1996) *Children's Literature Comes of Age; towards a new aesthetic*. New York: Garland

O'Grady, S. (1970) *Early Bardic Literature*. New York: Lemma Publishing

O'Sullivan, E. (1993) 'The fate of the Dual Addresses in the translation of children's literature' in *New Comparison*. 16. 109-119

Ogden, C.K. and Richards, I.A. (1923) *The Meaning of Meaning*. London: Routledge

Reddin, K. (1946) 'Children's Books in Ireland' in *The Irish Library Bulletin 7*

Rosen, M. (2000) 'Monologues and Spiels; the 'I' of my poems' in *Tales, Tellers and Texts*. eds. G. Cliff Hodges, M.J. Drummond and M. Styles. London: Cassell

Said, E.W. (1983) *The World, the Text and the Critic*. Cambridge MA: Harvard Unversity Press

Semprun, J. (1997) *Literature of Life*. London: Penguin

Stephens, J. (1992) *Language and Ideology in Children's Fiction*. London: Longman

Wall, B. (1991) *The Narrator's Voice; the dilemma of children's fiction*. London: Macmillan

Weaver, W. (1964) *Alice in Many Tongues*. Madison: University of Madison Press

Yeats, W.B. (1955) *Autobiographies*. London: Macmillan

Books for young people

Adler, D.A. (1993) *A Picture Book of Anne Frank*. New York: Holiday House

Agard, J. (1996) *Get Back, Pimple!* London: Viking Kestrel

Ahlberg, J. and A. (1981) *Peepo*. London: Viking Kestrel

Ahlberg, J. and A. (1982) *The Baby's Catalogue*. London: Viking Kestrel

Ahlberg, J. and A. (1988) *Starting School*. London: Viking Kestrel

Anderson, R. (1991) *Paper Faces*. Oxford University Press

Basile, G. (1632-34) *Il Pentamerone* (The Little Ones' Entertainment) English translation by Sir Richard Burton

Bawden, N. (1972) *Carrie's War*. London: Heinemann

Berry, J. (1988) *When I Dance*. London: Hamish Hamilton

Blake, J. (1997) *The Sandbag Secret*. London: Franklin Watts

Bloom, V. (1992) *Duppy Jamboree*. Cambridge University Press

Bordern, I. (1997) *The Little Ships*. London: Pavilion Books

Breinberg, P. and Lloyd, E. (1973) My Brother Sean. London: The Bodley Head

Breslin, T. (1995) *A Homecoming for Kezzie*. London: Methuen

Briggs, R. (1983) *When the Wind Blows*. Harmondsworth: Penguin

Briggs, R. (1984) *The Tin-Pot Foreign General and the Old Iron Woman*. London: Methuen

Briggs, R. (1998) *Ethel and Ernest, a true story*. London: Cape

Broad, R. and Fleming, S. (1981) *Nella's Last War*. Bristol: Falling Wall Press

Brown, F. (1960) *1856*. London: Dent

Browne, A. (1977) *A Walk in the Park*. London: Hamish Hamilton

Burningham, J. (1970) *Mr Grumpy's Outing*. London: Cape

Burningham, J. (1977) *Come Away From the Water, Shirley*. London: Cape

Burningham, J. (1998) *France*. London: Cape

Calvino, I. (1956) *Fiabe Italiane*. Rome: Einaudi

Carroll, L. (1865) *Alice's Adventures in Wonderland*. illus. J. Tenneil. London: Macmillan

Causeley, C. (1970) *Figgie Hobbin*. London: Macmillan

Charlton, M. (nd) *Tally Ho: the story of an Irish Hunter*. London: G. Putnam

Ciravegna, N. (1979) *Chichois de la rue des Mauvestis*. Paris: Bordas

Ciravegna, N. (1989) *Chichois et les copains du globe*. Paris: Bordas

Ciravegna, N. (1993) *Chichois et les histoires de France*. Paris: Bordas

Colum, P. (1916) *The King of Ireland's Son*. Edinburgh: Floris Books (1986)

Cruikshank, M. (1991) *Circling the Triangle*. Dublin: Poolbeg

Dillon, E. (1952) *The Last Island*. Dublin: O'Brien

Dillon, E. (1956) *The Island of Horses*. Harmondsworth: Penguin

Dillon, E. (1984) *The Lucky Bag*. Dublin: O'Brien

Dillon. E. (1990) *The Island of Ghosts*. Harmondsworth: Penguin

Dillon, E. (1991) *The Singing Cave*. Dublin: Poolbeg

Emmerich. E. (1991) *My children in Nazi Germany*. London: Wayland

Feeney, J. (1996) *Truths, Lies and Homework*. London: Penguin

Foreman, M. (1989) *War Boy*. London: Pavilion Books

Foreman, M. (1993) *War Game*. London: Pavilion Books

Foreman, M. (1997) *After the War Was Over*. London: Pavilion Books

Frank, A. (1947-1990) *Diary of Anne Frank*. London: Heinemann

Freil, M. (1993) *Charlie's Story*. Dublin: Poolbeg

Gaarder, J. (1997) *Hello! Is Anybody There?* trs. James Anderson. London: Orion

Gallas, C. (1985) *Rose Blanche*. London: Cape

Geras, A. (1995) *A Castle in the Dark*. London: A&C Black

Gibbons, A. (1996) *Street of Tall People*. London: Orion

Granfield, L. (1995) *In Flanders Fields*. London: Gollancz

Greenham, H. (1966) *Ann and Peter in Ireland*. London: Phoenix House

Hickey, T. (1989) *Where is Joe?* Dublin: Poolbeg

Hicylmazz, G. (1993) *The Frozen Waterfall*. London: Faber

Hoffman, M. and Binch, C. (1991) *Amazing Grace*. London: Frances Lincoln

Holm, A. (1965) *I Am David*. Harmondsworth: Puffin

Hughes, S. (1998) *The Lion and the Unicorn*. London: The Bodley Head

Hughes, T. (1992) *Rain Charm for the Duchy and other Laureate Poems*. London: Faber

Hughes, T. (1985) *Season Songs*. London: Faber

Hughes, T. (1995) *Collected Animal Poems* Vols. 1-5. London: Faber

Kay, J. (1999) *Two's Company*. London: Balckie

Keeping, C. (1974) *Railway Passage*. Oxford University Press

Keeping, C. (1984) *Sammy Streetsinger*. Oxford University Press

Keeping, C. (1989) *Adam and Paradise Island*. Oxford University Press

Kerr, J. (1971) *Out of the Hitler Time*. London: Harper Collins

Lenain, T. (1990) *Un pere pour la vie*. Paris: Hachette

Lenihan, E. (1993) *Fionn Mac Cumhail and the Baking Hags*. Cork: Mercier

Lenihan, E. (1997) *Gruesome Irish Tales for Children*. Cork: Mercier

Lenihan, E. (1998) *Humorous Irish Tales for Children*. Cork: Mercier

Lingard, J. (1991) *Tugs of War*. London: Hamish Hamilton

Lynch, P. (1934) *The Turf-cutter's Donkey*. Dublin: Poolbeg

Lynch, P. (1939) *The Grey Goose of Kilnevin*. Dublin: Poolbeg

Lynch, P. (1956) *The Bookshop on the Quay*. Dublin: Poolbeg

Lynch, P. (1953) *Brogreen and the Green Shoes*. Dublin: Poolbeg

MacRaois, C. (1988) *The Battle below Giltspur*. Dublin: Wolfhound

Magorian, M. (1981) *Goodnight Mister Tom*. London: Penguin

Marvici, T. (1983) *The Hiroshima Story*. London: A&C Black

Mauffret, Y. (1986) *Pepe la Boulange*. Paris: Ecole des Loisirs

McGough, R. and Rosen, M. (1979) You Tell Me. Harmondsworth: Puffin

McCaughren, T. (1994) *In Search of the Liberty Tree*. Dublin: Anvil

McCaughren, T. (1998) *Ride a Pale Horse*. Dublin: Anvil

Meade, L.T. (1897) *Wild Kitty*. London: W. and R. Chambers

Meade, L.T. (1902) *The Rebel of the School.* London: W. and R. Chambers

Milne (1224) *When We Were Very Young.* London: Methuen

Morgenstern, S. (1989) *Les Deux Moities de la Vie.* Paris: Rageot

Morpurgo, M. (1998) *Farm Boy.* London: Pavilion Books

Morpurgo, M. (1990) *Waiting for Anya.* London: Heinemann

Nerucci, G. (1880) *Sessanta Novelle Populari Montesi.* Le Monnier

Nichols, G. (1988) *Come On Into My Tropical Garden.* London: A&C Black

O'Sullivan, E. and Rosler, D. (1983) *I Like You, und du?* Frankfurt, Fischer

O'Laighleis, R. (1996) *Ecstasy and Other Stories.* Dublin: Poolbeg

O'Loughlin, L. (1997) *Fionn and the Scots Giant.* Dublin: Blackwater

O'Loughlin, L. (1997) *The Goba Soar.* Dublin: Blackwater

O'Loughlin, L. (1999) *The Salmon of Knowledge.* Dublin: Blackwater

Paton Walsh, J. (1994) *Knowledge of Angels.* Cambridge: Green Bay/Colt Books

Pausewang, G. (1996) *The Final Journey.* trans. P. Crampton. London: Viking

Pennac, D. (1992) *l'Evasion de Kamo.* Paris: Gallimard

Preussler, O. (1961) *The Little Water Sprite.* London: Abelard Schuman

Rowling, J.K. (1997) *Harry Potter and the Philosopher's Stone.* London: Bloomsbury

Richter, H.P. (1978) *Friedrich.* London: Heinemann

Rushdie, S. (1990) *Haroun and the Sea of Stories.* London: Penguin

Schami, R. and Gutschhahn, U. (1999) *Der geheime Bericht uber den Dichter Goethe.* Munich: Hanser

Schami, R. and Knorr, P. (1990) *Der Wunderkasten.* Weinheim: Betz

Schami, R. (1991) *A Handful of Stars.* trs. Rita Lesser. London: Penguin

Scott, M. (1991) *Windlord.* Dublin: Wolfhound

Scott, M. (1992) *Earthlord.* Dublin: Wolfhound

Scott, M. (1994) *Firelord.* Dublin: Wolfhound

Seraillier, I. (1956) *The Silver Sword.* London: Heinemann

Shea, P.D. (1995) *The Whispering Cloth.* Pennsylvania: Boyd Mills Press

Shemin, M. (1990) *The Little Riders.* London: Walker Books

Szpilman, W. (1999) *The Pianist.* London: Gollancz

Taylor, M. (1994) *Could This Be Love? I Wondered.* Dublin: O'Brien

Taylor, M. (1995) *Could I Love a Stranger?* Dublin: O'Brien

Westall, R. (1989) *Blitz Cat.* London: Methuen

Westall, R. (1990) *The Kingdom By the Sea.* London: Methuen

Westall, R. (1975) *The Machine Gunners.* London: Heinemann

Wild, M. (1991) *Let the Celebrations Begin.* London: Bodley Head

Zephaniah, B. (1994) *Funky Chickens.* London: Viking Kestrel

Zephaniah, B. (1995) *Talking Turkeys.* London: Viking Kestrel